LATIN VERB DRILLS

LATIN VERB DRILLS

Richard Prior

McGraw·Hill

New York   Chicago   San Francisco   Lisbon   London   Madrid   Mexico City
Milan   New Delhi   San Juan   Seoul   Singapore   Sydney   Toronto

1 2 3 4 5 6 7 8 9 0   VLP/VLP   0 9 8 7 6 5

ISBN 0-07-145395-4
Library of Congress Control Number: 2004116085

McGraw-Hill books are available at special quantity discounts to use as premiums and sales promotions, or for use in corporate training programs. For more information, please write to the Director of Special Sales, Professional Publishing, McGraw-Hill, Two Penn Plaza, New York, NY 10121-2298. Or contact your local bookstore.

This book is printed on acid-free paper.

Dis manibus

Contents

Preface

Latin Verb Drills is designed to be used as a review text and as a workbook for students of Latin at all levels, whether learning the language at school or studying it on their own. Teachers will also find *Latin Verb Drills* to be a useful supplement in the classroom.

The book is divided into fifteen chapters, each offering a concise review of a specific feature of the Latin verb system followed by exercises, which offer students opportunities to practice conjugation and translation from both Latin to English and English to Latin. In the back of the book there is a key to the exercises and an index of those verbs most commonly found in Latin literature.

I wish to extend thanks to Brian Lupo for his assistance in the preparation of this manuscript, and long overdue recognition to Ann Claire Felts.

LATIN VERB DRILLS

Overview of the Latin Verb System

Awareness of the characteristics of Latin verbs will help not only in seeing the overall structure of the Latin verb system, but also in learning, recognizing, and understanding forms in context.

Characteristics of Latin verbs

Latin verb forms can be described by the following five characteristics: person, number, tense, mood, and voice.

"Person" refers to the position of the speaker with respect to the subject of the verbs. There are three persons: first, second, and third.

First person is the speaker:

ego   I

Second person is the person being spoken to:

tū   you

Third person is the person or thing being spoken about:

is   he

"Number" refers to quantity. There are two numbers: singular (i.e., one) and plural (i.e., more than one). When describing verb forms, number is combined with person to show whether the speaker is alone or part of a group, whether only one person is being spoken to or a group is being addressed, and so on. Here is a chart showing how these two concepts work together:

	singular		*plural*	
first person	ego	I	nōs	we
second person	tū	you	vōs	you
third person	is	he	eī	they

Although Latin has personal pronouns to show the subject of a verb, they are unnecessary for understanding and provide only emphasis. In order to demonstrate person and number, Latin verbs rely on personal endings, which are attached to a verb's stem. For example, the personal ending -s signifies a second person singular subject (i.e., **tū**), and so the verb **portās** means "you carry," even if the pronoun **tū** does not accompany it. Personal endings also convey voice (see below).

"Tense" refers to another matrix, specifically the intersection between time and aspect. For a Latin verb, time can be now, earlier, or later. The term "aspect" refers to how a speaker views an action, either as a thing in process (called "the continuous aspect" or "the present system") or as a thing completed (called "the completed aspect" or "the perfect system"). Latin has six tenses: present, imperfect, future, perfect, pluperfect, and future perfect. Here is how time and aspect come together to form them.

time	**aspect**	
	continuous	*completed*
now	present	perfect
earlier	imperfect	pluperfect
later	future	future perfect

"Mood" refers to the way the speaker treats an action. There are three moods: indicative, imperative, and subjunctive.

Indicative mood treats an action as a fact.

Imperative mood treats an action as a command.

Subjunctive mood treats an action as an idea or wish.

"Voice" refers to the relationship between the subject and the verb. Voice is indicated by personal endings. There are three voices: active, middle, and passive.

Active voice is used when the subject performs the action.

Middle voice shows the subject performing an action to itself or for its own benefit or interest.

Passive voice is used when the subject receives the action.

The conjugations

Latin verbs are divided into four main groups called "conjugations." The groups are formed by common characteristics, namely that of a theme vowel. The conjugation of a verb can be recognized by its infinitive, which appears as the second principal part in its dictionary listing:

first conjugation	-āre
second conjugation	-ēre
third conjugation	-ere
fourth conjugation	-īre

Also, a few verbs are called "irregular" because they do not fall into any of the four regular conjugations.

Principal parts

Latin verbs have either three or four principal parts. They are given in the dictionary listing for every verb and are roughly analogous to English verb listings such as "drink, drank, drunk" and so on. For this English example, "drink" is the present tense form, "drank" the past tense form, and "drunk" the past participle. Here is an example of the principal parts of a Latin verb:

bibō, bibere, bibī, bibitum

The first part (**bibō**) is the first person singular, present indicative active ("I drink"). The second part (**bibere**) is the present infinitive active ("to drink"). These first two parts are all one needs to create all the forms of the present system active and passive, plus a few other forms.

The third part (**bibī**) is the same as the first part, except it is the "perfect" version—that is to say, it is the first person singular, perfect indicative active ("I drank"). It provides all the information you need to form all the perfect system tenses, but only in active voice.

The fourth part (**bibitum**) also plays a role in the perfect system. The perfect passive participle is formed from it, which is needed for the perfect passive tenses.

The fourth part is also a bit problematic in that different traditions list different things for it. In this book the fourth part shows the supine form with the ending **-um**. Other books may list the perfect passive participle with the ending **-us**, or sometimes the future active participle with the ending **-ūrus**. Some verbs have no fourth principal part. This is especially true for intransitive verbs. In the case of deponent verbs, the third principal part already conveys this information, so a fourth part does not need to be included. The important thing that these two traditions share is the base form, or what is left when the **-um** or **-us** is removed.

Present Indicative Active

First and Second Conjugations

The present tense shows an action in the process of happening in present time. Latin has one way to express this, whereas English has three:

	you carry
portās	you do carry
	you are carrying

The present tense in Latin has a distinct form in each of the four conjugations. It is the only tense for which this is true. In addition, it is the only tense in which irregular verbs manifest their irregularity. Because of this it is vital to know to which conjugation a verb belongs.

A verb's conjugation can be recognized by its infinitive, which appears as the second principal part. All Latin verbs whose second principal part ends in **-āre** are called "first conjugation" and so on, as the following chart shows:

first conjugation	portō, port**āre**, portāvī, portātum
second conjugation	moneō, mon**ēre**, monuī, monitum
third conjugation	mittō, mitt**ere**, mīsī, missum
fourth conjugation	sentiō, sent**īre**, sensī, sensum

Note that the theme vowel of second conjugation is a long **e**, while that of third conjugation is a short **e**. This is a very important difference!

Present tense

First and second conjugation verbs are similar in their formation of present tense; variation lies in their theme vowel.

first conjugation: *portō, portāre, portāvī, portātum*

portō	I carry, I do carry, I am carrying
portās	you carry, you do carry, you are carrying
portat	he/she/it carries, he/she/it does carry, he/she/it is carrying
portāmus	we carry, we do carry, we are carrying
portātis	you carry, you do carry, you are carrying
portant	they carry, they do carry, they are carrying

second conjugation: *moneō, monēre, monuī, monitum*

moneō	I warn, I do warn, I am warning
monēs	you warn, you do warn, you are warning
monet	he/she/it warns, he/she/it does warn, he/she/it is warning
monēmus	we warn, we do warn, we are warning
monētis	you warn, you do warn, you are warning
monent	they warn, they do warn, they are warning

Each conjugation maintains its theme vowel throughout, with one exception. For the first person singular of first conjugation verbs, the theme vowel **-ā-** is contracted into the personal ending **-ō**.

common first conjugation verbs
agitō, agitāre, agitāvī, agitātum, to agitate, think about, get something going
ambulō, ambulāre, ambulāvī, ambulātum, to walk
amō, amāre, amāvī, amātum, to like, love
appellō, appellāre, appellāvī, appellātum, to call (often by name)
armō, armāre, armāvī, armātum, to equip with weapons
cantō, cantāre, cantāvī, cantātum, to sing, play (an instrument)
celebrō, celebrāre, celebrāvī, celebrātum, to visit often, make well known
certō, certāre, certāvī, certātum, to struggle, decide by contest
cessō, cessāre, cessāvī, cessātum, to do nothing, slack off
cōgitō, cōgitāre, cōgitāvī, cōgitātum, to think, ponder
comparō, comparāre, comparāvī, comparātum, to prepare, buy, furnish
constō, constāre, constitī, constātum, to stand together, stand still, stop
creō, creāre, creāvī, creātum, to create, elect
cūrō, cūrāre, cūrāvi, cūrātum, to take care of
dō, dare, dedī, datum, to give
donō, donāre, donāvī, donātum, to give (as a gift)
dubitō, dubitāre, dubitāvī, dubitātum, to hesitate, doubt
errō, errāre, errāvī, errātum, to wander, be wrong

existimō, existimāre, existimāvī, existimātum, to think, judge, evaluate

exspectō, exspectāre, exspectāvī, exspectātum, to wait for

habitō, habitāre, habitāvī, habitātum, to live, dwell, inhabit

ignōrō, ignōrāre, ignōrāvī, ignōrātum, to not know

imperō, imperāre, imperāvī, imperātum, to give an order (with dative)

indicō, indicāre, indicāvī, indicātum, to make known, betray

intrō, intrāre, intrāvī, intrātum, to enter

iūrō, iūrāre, iūrāvī, iūrātum, to swear

iuvō, iuvāre, iūvī, iūtum, to help, please

laborō, laborāre, laborāvī, laborātum, to work, suffer

laudō, laudāre, laudāvī, laudātum, to praise

lavō, lavāre, lāvī, lautum *or* lavātum *or* lōtum, to wash

līberō, līberāre, līberāvī, līberātum, to set free

mandō, mandāre, mandāvī, mandātum, to entrust, order

memorō, memorāre, memorāvī, memorātum, to remind, mention

monstrō, monstrāre, monstrāvī, monstrātum, to show

mutō, mutāre, mutāvī, mutātum, to change, move

narrō, narrāre, narrāvī, narrātum, to tell (in story form)

nāvigō, nāvigāre, nāvigāvī, nāvigātum, to sail

necō, necāre, necāvī, necātum, to kill

negō, negāre, negāvī, negātum, to deny, say no

nōminō, nōmināre, nōmināvī, nōminātum, to name, mention

nuntiō, nuntiāre, nuntiāvī, nuntiātum, to announce

occupō, occupāre, occupāvī, occupātum, to seize

optō, optāre, optāvī, optātum, to choose

ornō, ornāre, ornāvī, ornātum, to decorate

ōrō, ōrāre, ōrāvī, ōrātum, to beg, ask, speak, pray

parō, parāre, parāvī, parātum, to get ready, obtain, prepare

portō, portāre, portāvī, portātum, to carry, bring

postulō, postulāre, postulāvī, postulātum, to demand

properō, properāre, properāvī, properātum, to hurry

pugnō, pugnāre, pugnāvī, pugnātum, to fight

putō, putāre, putāvī, putātum, to think, value

regnō, regnāre, regnāvī, regnātum, to rule

revocō, recovāre, revocāvī, recovātum, to call back

rogō, rogāre, rogāvī, rogātum, to ask

simulō, simulāre, simulāvī, simulātum, to pretend

sonō, sonāre, sonuī, sonitum, to make a sound

spectō, spectāre, spectāvī, spectātum, to watch

spērō, spērāre, spērāvī, spērātum, to expect, hope

spīrō, spīrāre, spīrāvī, spīrātum, to breathe

stō, stāre, stetī, statum, to stand, stay

superō, superāre, superāvī, superātum, to overcome, conquer

temptō, temptāre, temptāvī, temptātum, to try, test

vetō, vetāre, vetuī, vetitum, to deny, say no

vigilō, vigilāre, vigilāvī, vigilātum, to be awake, watch

vocō, vocāre, vocāvī, vocātum, to call, summon

volō, volāre, volāvī, volātum, to fly

common second conjugation verbs

ardeō, ardēre, arsī, arsum, to burn, be on fire

audeō, audēre, ausus sum, to dare

augeō, augēre, auxī, auctum, to increase, enlarge

careō, carēre, caruī, caritūrus, to lack, be without (uses an ablative object)

caveō, cavēre, cāvī, cautum, to beware, be on guard

contineō, continēre, continuī, contentum, to hold together, contain

debeō, debēre, debuī, debitum, to owe; ought, should, must

decet, decēre, decuīt (impersonal), it is right, fitting, proper

dēleō, dēlēre, dēlēvī, dēlētum, to destroy

doceō, docēre, docuī, doctum, to teach

doleō, dolēre, doluī, dolitum, to feel pain, to cause pain

exerceō, exercēre, exercuī, exercitum, to make strong, train, harass

fleō, flēre, flēvī, flētum, to weep

habeō, habēre, habuī, habitum, to have, hold, consider, regard

horreō, horrēre, horruī, to bristle

iaceō, iacēre, iacuī, to recline, lie

impleō, implēre, implēvī, implētum, to fill up

iubeō, iubēre, iussī, iussum, to order

lateō, latēre, latuī, to lie hidden

maneō, manēre, mansī, mansum, to stay

mereō, merēre, meruī, meritum, to deserve, earn

misceō, miscēre, miscuī, mixtum, to mix

moneō, monēre, monuī, monitum, to warn, advise

moveō, movēre, mōvī, mōtum, to move

noceō, nocēre, nocuī, nocitum, to harm, be harmful (with dative)

paenitet, paenitēre, paenituit (impersonal), to regret (with genitive)

pāreō, pārēre, pāruī, pāritum, to be obedient, obey

pateō, patēre, patuī, to lie open, exposed

persuadeō, persuadēre, persuasī, persuasum, to persuade (with dative)

placeō, placēre, placuī, placitum, to please (with dative)

praebeō, praebēre, praebuī, praebitum, to offer

respondeō, respondēre, respondī, responsum, to answer, correspond (usually with dative)

retineō, retinēre, retinuī, retentum, to hold back, keep

rīdeō, rīdēre, rīsī, rīsum, to laugh, smile

sedeō, sedēre, sēdī, sessum, to sit, stay put

soleō, solēre, solitus sum, to be in the habit of doing something, usually do something

studeō, studēre, studuī, to be eager, be busy with (usually with dative)

sustineō, sustinēre, sustinuī, sustentum, to support, uphold

taceō, tacēre, tacuī, tacitum, to be quiet

teneō, tenēre, tenuī, tentum, to hold, have

terreō, terrēre, terruī, territum, to scare

timeō, timēre, timuī, to be afraid, fear

valeō, valēre, valuī, valitum, to be strong

videō, vidēre, vīdī, vīsum, to see; (passive voice) to seem, be seen

Exercise 2.1

Conjugate the following verbs in present tense.

1. **spērō, spērāre, spērāvī, spērātum**, to expect, hope

   ego _____   nōs _____

   tū _____   vōs _____

   is _____   eī _____

2. **vocō, vocāre, vocāvī, vocātum**, to call, summon

   ego _____   nōs _____

   tū _____   vōs _____

   is _____   eī _____

3. **sustineō, sustinēre, sustinuī, sustentum**, to support, uphold

   ego _____   nōs _____

   tū _____   vōs _____

   is _____   eī _____

4. **praebeō, praebēre, praebuī, praebitum**, to offer

   ego _____   nōs _____

   tū _____   vōs _____

   is _____   eī _____

Exercise 2.2

Write the present tense forms of the following verbs to agree with the subject provided.

1. nōs (laudāre) _____
2. tū (iacēre) _____
3. vōs (latēre) _____
4. eī (volāre) _____
5. eī (cantāre) _____
6. vōs (indicāre) _____
7. ego (nomināre) _____
8. vōs (optāre) _____
9. ego (putāre) _____
10. ego (mandāre) _____
11. tū (ornāre) _____
12. nōs (memorāre) _____
13. is (terrēre) _____
14. is (merēre) _____
15. vōs (expectāre) _____
16. is (habēre) _____
17. nōs (vetāre) _____
18. ego (patēre) _____
19. vōs (dubitāre) _____
20. tū (existimāre) _____

Exercise 2.3

Translate the following verbs into English.

1. parat _____
2. lavant _____
3. nāvigant _____
4. nocent _____
5. dēlētis _____
6. placent _____

7. portās _____

8. solent _____

9. cessat _____

10. rogō _____

11. vigilat _____

12. cūrat _____

13. laborās _____

14. monstrātis _____

15. regnat _____

16. respondeō _____

17. spērat _____

18. habitātis _____

19. manet _____

20. revocant _____

Exercise 2.4

Translate the following verbs into Latin using the vocabulary provided.

1. they are giving (**dare**) _____

2. he changes (**mutāre**) _____

3. you (sing.) are killing (**necāre**) _____

4. we demand (**postulāre**) _____

5. you (sing.) walk (**ambulāre**) _____

6. you (pl.) are teaching (**docēre**) _____

7. they give (**donāre**) _____

8. you (sing.) are calling (**vocāre**) _____

9. we are standing (**stāre**) _____

10. we keep (**retinēre**) _____

3

Present Indicative Active
Third and Fourth Conjugations

Third conjugation

Third conjugation verbs, such as **mittō**, **mitt*ere***, **mīsī**, **missum**, can be identified by the short **-ere** ending in their second principal part. When conjugated in present tense, the short **e** weakens and a new vowel pattern emerges.

third conjugation: *mittō, mittere, mīsī, missum*

mitt**ō**	I send, I do send, I am sending
mitt**is**	you send, you do send, you are sending
mitt**it**	he/she/it sends, he/she/it does send, he/she/it is sending
mitt**imus**	we send, we do send, we are sending
mitt**itis**	you send, you do send, you are sending
mitt**unt**	they send, they do send, they are sending

There is a variant group of third conjugation verbs called "third conjugation **-iō**" verbs, such as **cap*iō***, **cap*ere***, **cēpī**, **captum**. They can be recognized by the first principal part ending in **-iō**, but with the second principal part still ending in **-ere**, which is why they are still considered third conjugation. The distinguishing feature of these verbs is that wherever regular third conjugation verbs do not have an **i**, **-iō** verbs add one. There are only a few forms where this **i** is not apparent, one of which being the present infinitive active (i.e., the second principal part). Compare this **-iō** verb to the regular third conjugation verb **mittō** above. Pay special attention to the first person singular and the third person plural forms.

third conjugation -*iō*: *capiō, capere, cēpī, captum*

cap**iō**	I take, I do take, I am taking
cap**is**	you take, you do take, you are taking

capit	he/she/it takes, he/she/it does take, he/she/it is taking
capimus	we take, we do take, we are taking
capitis	you take, you do take, you are taking
capiunt	they take, they do take, they are taking

Fourth conjugation

Fourth conjugation verbs, such as **sentiō**, **sentīre**, **sensī**, **sensum**, are easily recognized by their second principal part ending in **-īre**. In present tense formation they are virtually identical to third conjugation **-iō** verbs; the only differences appear in the second person singular, and the first and second persons plural. In those forms the theme vowel, **i**, is long rather than short.

fourth conjugation: *sentiō*, *sentīre*, *sensī*, *sensum*

sentiō	I feel, I do feel, I am feeling
sentīs	you feel, you do feel, you are feeling
sentit	he/she/it feels, he/she/it does feel, he/she/it is feeling
sentīmus	we feel, we do feel, we are feeling
sentītis	you feel, you do feel, you are feeling
sentiunt	they feel, they do feel, they are feeling

common third conjugation verbs

accēdō, accēdere, accessī, accessum, to approach, go near (with *ad* or *in* and the accusative)

accidō, accidere, accidī, to happen, fall down, ask for help

addō, addere, addidī, additum, to add, give to

agō, agere, ēgī, actum, to do, drive, lead, be busy

alō, alere, aluī, altum, to cherish, nourish

āmittō, āmittere, āmīsī, āmissum, to send away, let go, lose

appāreō, appārēre, appāruī, appāritum, to appear

ascendō, ascendere, ascendī, ascensum, to climb, go up

bibō, bibere, bibī, bibitum, to drink

cadō, cadere, cecidī, cāsum, to fall

caedō, caedere, cecīdī, caesum, to cut, kill

canō, canere, cecinī, cantum, to sing, play (an instrument)

cēdō, cēdere, cessī, cessum, to go, withdraw, yield

cernō, cerere, crēvī, crētum, to separate, distinguish, pick out

cingō, cingere, cinxī, cinctum, to surround, wrap

claudō, claudere, clausī, clausum, to close, conclude

cognoscō, cognoscere, cognōvī, cognitum, to learn; (in the perfect system) to know

cōgō, cōgere, coēgī, coactum, to compel, gather, drive, force

colligō, colligere, collēgī, collectum, to gather, collect

colō, colere, coluī, cultum, to pay attention to, nurture, cultivate

comedō, comedere, comēdī, comēsum *or* comestum, to eat up

committō, committere, commīsī, commissum, to connect, combine; entrust

condō, condere, condidī, condītum, to found, build; put in safe keeping, hide

constituō, constituere, constituī, constitūtum, to stand or set something up, decide

consulō, consulere, consuluī, consultum, to consult

contemnō, contemnere, contempsī, contemptum, to despise

contendō, contendere, contendī, contentum, to strain, hurry, fight

crēdō, crēdere, crēdidī, crēditum, to trust, rely on, believe (usually with dative)

crescō, crescere, crēvī, crētum, to grow

currō, currere, cucurrī, cursum, to run

dēfendō, dēfendere, dēfendī, dēfensum, to defend, drive off

descendō, descendere, descendī, descensum, to climb down

dīcō, dīcere, dīxī, dīctum, to tell, say

dīligō, dīligere, dīlexī, dīlectum, to love, esteem, pick out

discedō, discedere, discessī, discessum, to leave, separate

discō, discere, didicī, to learn

dīvidō, dīvidere, dīvīsī, dīvīsum, to divide

dūcō, dūcere, duxī, ductum, to take someone someplace, lead

emō, emere, ēmī, emptum, to buy

exuō, exuere, exuī, exūtum, to strip

fallō, fallere, fefellī, falsum, to deceive

fīgō, fīgere, fixī, fixum, to fasten, affix

fingō, fingere, finxī, fictum, to shape, form

fluō, fluere, fluxī, fluxum, to flow

frangō, frangere, frēgī, fractum, to break

fundō, fundere, fūdī, fūsum, to pour

gerō, gerere, gessī, gestum, to carry, wage, accomplish

gignō, gignere, genuī, genitum, to give birth, cause

impōnō, impōnere, imposuī, impositum, to put upon

induō, induere, induī, indūtum, to put on, dress

instituō, instituere, instituī, institūtum, to set up, instruct, decide

instruō, instruere, instruxī, instructum, to build, equip

intellegō, intellegere, intellexī, intellectum, to understand, be aware of, appreciate

intendō, intendere, intendī, intentum, to stretch, intend, aim at

invideō, invidēre, invīdī, invīsum, to cast the evil eye; envy (with dative) iungō, iungere, iunxī, iunctum, to join, connect

laedō, laedere, laesī, laesum, to hurt

legō, legere, lēgī, lectum, to choose, pick, gather, read

lūdō, lūdere, lūsī, lūsum, to play, deceive

metuō, metuere, metuī, metūtum, to fear

mittō, mittere, mīsī, missum, to send, release, throw, to make something go away under
    its own power

neglegō, neglegere, neglexī, neglectum, to neglect

noscō, noscere, nōvi, nōtum, to learn; (in perfect system) to know, recognize

occīdo, occīdere, occīdī, occīsum, to kill

occurro, occurrere, occurrī, occursum, to meet (with dative)

ostendō, ostendere, ostendī, ostentum, to show

pandō, pandere, pandī, pansum *or* passum, to open up, stretch

parcō, parcere, pepercī, parsum, to spare, be sparing (with dative)

pellō, pellere, pepulī, pulsum, to push, drive

pendō, pendere, pependī, pensum, to hang, weigh, pay

perdō, perdere, perdidī, perditum, to lose, destroy, waste

pergō, pergere, perrexī, perrectum, to continue

permittō, permittere, permīsī, permissum, to allow, send through, throw

petō, petere, petiī *or* petīvī, petītum, to look for, ask, head for, attack

pōnō, pōnere, posuī, positum, to put, lay

premō, premere, pressī, pressum, to press, push

prōdō, prōdere, prōdidī, prōditum, to betray, hand over

prōmittō, prōmittere, prōmīsī, prōmissum, to promise, send ahead

quaerō, quaerere, quaesiī *or* quaesīvī, quaesītum, to look for, ask

quiescō, quiescere, quiēvī, quiētum, to rest

reddō, reddere, reddidī, redditum, to give back, surrender, repeat

regō, regere, rexī, rectum, to rule, guide

relinquō, relinquere, relīquī, relictum, to abandon, leave

requīrō, requīrere, requīsiī *or* requīsīvī, requīsītum, to demand, ask, look for

revertō, revertere, revertī, reversum, to turn back

rumpō, rumpere, rūpī, ruptum, to break, burst

scindō, scindere, scidī, scissum, to cut

scrībō, scrībere, scripsī, scriptum, to write, draw

sinō, sinere, sīvī, situm, to let, allow

solvō, solvere, solvī, solūtum, to loosen, untie, pay

spargō, spargere, sparsī, sparsum, to scatter, sprinkle

spernō, spernere, sprēvī, sprētum, to reject, scorn

statuō, statuere, statuī, statūtum, to set up, stop, decide

sternō, sternere, strāvī, strātum, to spread, stretch

sūmō, sūmere, sumpsī, sumptum, to take, assume

surgō, surgere, surrexī, surrectum, to rise

tangō, tangere, tetigī, tactum, to touch

tegō, tegere, texī, tectum, to cover

tendō, tendere, tetendī, tentum *or* tensum, to stretch, try

tollō, tollere, sustulī, sublātum, to raise, carry away, destroy

trādō, trādere, trādidī, trāditum, to hand over, surrender

trahō, trahere, traxī, tractum, to pull, drag

vehō, vehere, vexī, vectum, to carry; to ride (middle voice with ablative)

vendō, vendere, vendidī, venditum, to sell

vertō, vertere, vertī, versum, to turn

vincō, vincere, vīcī, victum, to conquer

vīvō, vīvere, vixī, victum, to live

common third conjugation *-iō* verbs

accipiō, accipere, accēpī, acceptum, to welcome, receive

aspiciō, aspicere, aspexī, aspectum, to look at

capiō, capere, cēpī, captum, to take, catch

conficiō, conficere, confēcī, confectum, to finish

cōniciō, cōnicere, cōniēcī, cōniectum, to hurl

cupiō, cupere, cupīvī, cupītum, to desire, long for

effugiō, effugere, effūgī, to escape

ēripiō, ēripere, ēripuī, ēreptum, to grab, take out violently

excipiō, excipere, excēpī, exceptum, to take out, take up, catch, receive

faciō, facere, fēci, factum, to make, do

fugiō, fugere, fūgī, fugitum, to run away, flee

iaciō, iacere, iēcī, iactum, to throw

incipiō, incipere, incēpī, inceptum, to begin

interficiō, interficere, interfēcī, interfectum, to kill

pariō, parere, peperī, partum, to give birth, produce

percutiō, percutere, percussī, percussum, to hit, strike

perficiō, perficere, perfēcī, perfectum, to complete

rapiō, rapere, rapuī, raptum, to take (forcefully)

recipiō, recipere, recēpī, receptum, to accept, take back

respiciō, respicere, respexī, respectum, to look back

suscipiō, suscipere, suscēpī, susceptum, to undertake, accept

common fourth conjugation verbs

aperiō, aperīre, aperuī, apertum, to open, uncover

audiō, audīre, audīvī, audītum, to hear, listen

custōdiō, custōdīre, custōdiī *or* custōdīvī, custōditum, to guard

dormiō, dormīre, dormīvī, dormītum, to sleep

ēveniō, ēvenīre, ēvēnī, ēventum, to come out, result

fīniō, fīnīre, fīnīvī, fīnītum, to finish

inveniō, invenīre, invēnī, inventum, to come upon, find

mūniō, mūnīre, mūniī, mūnītum, to fortify

nesciō, nescīre, nescīvī, nescītum, to not know

perveniō, pervenīre, pervēnī, perventum, to arrive

reperiō, reperīre, repperī, repertum, to find

sciō, scīre, scīvī, scītum, to know

sentiō, sentīre, sensī, sensum, to feel, perceive, experience, realize

sepeliō, sepelīre, sepeliī *or* sepelīvī, sepultum, to bury

serviō, servīre, servīvī, servītum (with dative), to be a slave, serve

veniō, venīre, vēnī, ventum, to come

Exercise 3.1

Conjugate the following verbs in present tense.

1. **canō, canere, cecinī, cantum**, to sing, play (an instrument)

   ego _____   nōs _____

   tū _____   vōs _____

   is _____   eī _____

2. **currō, currere, cucurrī, cursum**, to run

   ego _____   nōs _____

   tū _____   vōs _____

   is _____   eī _____

3. **accipiō, accipere, accēpī, acceptum**, to welcome, receive

   ego _____   nōs _____

   tū _____   vōs _____

   is _____   eī _____

4. **conficiō, conficere, confēcī, confectum**, to finish

   ego _____   nōs _____

   tū _____   vōs _____

   is _____   eī _____

5. **inveniō**, **invenīre**, **invēnī**, **inventum**, to come upon, find

ego _____ nōs _____

tū _____ vōs _____

is _____ eī _____

Exercise 3.2

Write the forms of the following verbs to agree with the subject provided.

1. tū (aspicere) _____

2. ego (crescere) _____

3. vōs (claudere) _____

4. tū (regere) _____

5. is (noscere) _____

6. eī (cadere) _____

7. vōs (consulere) _____

8. is (caedere) _____

9. nōs (mittere) _____

10. ego (revertere) _____

11. tū (contemnere) _____

12. ego (fundere) _____

13. is (colere) _____

14. vōs (vincere) _____

15. nōs (fingere) _____

16. eī (conficere) _____

17. eī (gerere) _____

18. nōs (neglegere) _____

19. is (accidere) _____

20. is (petere) _____

Exercise 3.3

Translate the following verbs into English.

1. vendit _____
2. cingunt _____
3. alit _____
4. rapiunt _____
5. scrībō _____
6. effugit _____
7. pergit _____
8. custōdītis _____
9. iungō _____
10. pandunt _____
11. āmittimus _____
12. fluit _____
13. invidēmus _____
14. discedit _____
15. emit _____
16. pōnunt _____
17. fīniō _____
18. mūniunt _____
19. parcimus _____
20. recipis _____

Exercise 3.4

Translate the following verbs into Latin using the vocabulary provided.

1. he abandons (**relinquere**) _____
2. I put (**impōnere**) _____
3. we are arriving (**pervenīre**) _____
4. you (pl.) are leading (**ducere**) _____
5. they attach (**fīgere**) _____

6. they are throwing (**iacere**) _____

7. they scatter (**spargere**) _____

8. you (sing.) live (**vīvere**) _____

9. I am coming (**venīre**) _____

10. we grab (**ēripere**) _____

11. they climb down (**descendere**) _____

12. you (sing.) are breaking (**frangere**) _____

4

Imperfect Indicative Active

The imperfect is the past time tense for the continuous aspect. It shows an action that was in the process of happening in the past, happened repeatedly in the past, or even began in the past and may or may not be continuing in the present. There are many ways to translate the imperfect.

portābant	they were carrying
	they used to carry
	they kept carrying
	they began to carry
	they carried (if it happened more than once)

The imperfect tense is one of the easiest Latin verb tenses to form and recognize. It merely inserts the tense indicator **-ba-** between the verb stem and the personal ending. This tense indicator is the same for all conjugations.

portābam	monēbam	mittēbam	capiēbam	sentiēbam
portābās	monēbās	mittēbās	capiēbās	sentiēbās
portābat	monēbat	mittēbat	capiēbat	sentiēbat
portābāmus	monēbāmus	mittēbāmus	capiēbāmus	sentiēbāmus
portābātis	monēbātis	mittēbātis	capiēbātis	sentiēbātis
portābant	monēbant	mittēbant	capiēbant	sentiēbant

There are two items of note. First, the personal ending for the first person singular is **-m** instead of **-ō**. Second, the verb stem to which the tense indicator **-ba-** is attached for third conjugation **-iō** and fourth conjugation verbs is the same: **-iē-**.

Exercise 4.1

Conjugate the following verbs in imperfect tense.

1. **impōnō**, **impōnere**, **imposuī**, **impositum**, to put upon

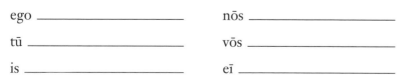

ego _____   nōs _____

tū _____   vōs _____

is _____   eī _____

2. **sciō, scīre, scīvī, scītum**, to know

ego _____   nōs _____

tū _____   vōs _____

is _____   eī _____

3. **regnō, regnāre, regnāvī, regnātum**, to rule

ego _____   nōs _____

tū _____   vōs _____

is _____   eī _____

4. **noceō, nocēre, nocuī, nocitum**, to harm

ego _____   nōs _____

tū _____   vōs _____

is _____   eī _____

Exercise 4.2

Write the forms of the following verbs in imperfect tense to agree with the subject provided.

1. is (comparāre) _____

2. eī (intrāre) _____

3. vōs (mittere) _____

4. is (movēre) _____

5. vōs (nescīre) _____

6. ego (condere) _____

7. tū (imperāre) _____

8. is (mūnīre) _____

9. nōs (sepelīre) _____

10. ego (claudere) _____

11. nōs (stāre) _____

12. tū (dūcere) _____

13. eī (intendere) _____

14. eī (rīdēre) _____

15. ego (permittere) _____

16. nōs (scrībere) _____

17. vōs (superāre) _____

18. tū (committere) _____

19. eī (fluere) _____

20. is (negāre) _____

Exercise 4.3

Translate the following verbs into English.

1. negābant _____

2. canēbat _____

3. iaciēbātis _____

4. percutiēbam _____

5. implēbās _____

6. laudābātis _____

7. sperābat _____

8. pārēbam _____

9. spīrābat _____

10. perdēbātis _____

11. lūdēbat _____

12. nocēbant _____

13. occurrēbat _____

14. parābātis _____

15. properābam _____

16. mandābāmus _____

17. necābātis _____

18. legēbat _____

19. solvēbāmus _____

20. consulēbātis _____

Exercise 4.4

Translate the following verbs into Latin using the vocabulary provided.

1. you (pl.) were stopping (**statuere**) _____

2. you (sing.) were adding (**addere**) _____

3. we used to owe (**debēre**) _____

4. you (sing.) used to love (**dīligere**) _____

5. he was giving (**donāre**) _____

6. you (pl.) were promising (**promittere**) _____

7. it used to result (**ēvenīre**) _____

8. they were calling back (**revocāre**) _____

9. I was hesitating (**dubitāre**) _____

10. I was welcoming (**accipere**) _____

5

Future Indicative Active

The future tense, as its name implies, describes an action that takes place in the future. The meaning of **portābimus**, then, is simply "we will carry," or "we will be carrying." The future tense is formed two different ways: one for first and second conjugation verbs, and another for third, third **-iō**, and fourth.

First and second conjugation verbs use a tense indicator somewhat similar to the imperfect tense. The first person singular ending for the future tense for first and second conjugation verbs is **-ō**.

portā**bō**	monē**bō**
portā**bis**	monē**bis**
portā**bit**	monē**bit**
portā**bimus**	monē**bimus**
portā**bitis**	monē**bitis**
portā**bunt**	monē**bunt**

It is also useful to note that the vowel pattern here (**ō, i, i, i, i, u**) is the same pattern seen in the present tense of third conjugation verbs.

Third, third **-iō**, and fourth conjugation verbs indicate future tense in a very different way.

mitt**am**	cap**iam**	sent**iam**
mitt**ēs**	cap**iēs**	sent**iēs**
mitt**et**	cap**iet**	sent**iet**
mitt**ēmus**	cap**iēmus**	sent**iēmus**
mitt**ētis**	cap**iētis**	sent**iētis**
mitt**ent**	cap**ient**	sent**ient**

Note that all but one of the future tense forms for third conjugation verbs is identical to the present tense forms for second conjugation. Also note that third **-iō** and fourth conjugation verbs show the additional **-i-** before the endings used in regular third conjugation.

Exercise 5.1

Conjugate the following verbs in future tense.

1. **aperiō, aperīre, aperuī, apertum**, to open, uncover

   ego _____   nōs _____

   tū _____   vōs _____

   is _____   eī _____

2. **mereō, merēre, meruī, meritum**, to deserve, earn

   ego _____   nōs _____

   tū _____   vōs _____

   is _____   eī _____

3. **pugnō, pugnāre, pugnāvī, pugnātum**, to fight

   ego _____   nōs _____

   tū _____   vōs _____

   is _____   eī _____

4. **ascendō, ascendere, ascendī, ascensum**, to climb, go up

   ego _____   nōs _____

   tū _____   vōs _____

   is _____   eī _____

Exercise 5.2

Write the forms of the following verbs in future tense to agree with the subject provided.

1. vōs (dormīre) _____

2. eī (rogāre) _____

3. ego (vīvere) _____

4. nōs (ignorāre) _____

5. eī (augēre) _____

6. nōs (discedere) _____

7. is (intellegere) _____

8. ego (noscere) _____

9. vōs (quaerere) _____

10. nōs (neglegere) _____

11. is (regere) _____

12. nōs (cernere) _____

13. ego (pervenīre) _____

14. vōs (cognoscere) _____

15. nōs (spargere) _____

16. ego (accipere) _____

17. is (defendere) _____

18. vōs (dolēre) _____

19. nōs (horrēre) _____

20. eī (continēre) _____

Exercise 5.3

Translate the following verbs into English.

1. gerent _____

2. ambulābimus _____

3. monēbō _____

4. cantābitis _____

5. indicābitis _____

6. emet _____

7. manēbit _____

8. bibēmus _____

9. cēdētis _____

10. interficiēs _____

11. revertet _____

12. aperiēs _____

13. constituent _____

14. habēbitis _____

15. rapiam _____

16. putābit _____

17. accēdent _____

18. agam _____

19. instruent _____

20. pugnābimus _____

Exercise 5.4

Translate the following verbs into Latin using the vocabulary provided.

1. he will climb (**ascendere**) _____

2. they will throw (**cōnicere**) _____

3. I will hurt (**laedere**) _____

4. they will deserve (**merēre**) _____

5. we will take (**sūmere**) _____

6. you (sing.) will wait for (**expectāre**) _____

7. we will set free (**līberāre**) _____

8. they will demand (**postulāre**) _____

9. you (pl.) will hold back (**retinēre**) _____

10. they will look at (**aspicere**) _____

The Perfect System Active

As the present, imperfect, and future tenses are the tenses of the continuous aspect, also called "the present system," the perfect, pluperfect, and future perfect tenses are the tenses of the completed aspect, also called "the perfect system."

Where the continuous aspect emphasizes actions in progress, the completed aspect (the perfect system) stresses the completion of an action.

The first and second principal parts of a verb provide all the information one needs to form the tenses of the present system. The third and fourth principal parts provide what is needed to form the tenses of the perfect system.

The forms of the perfect system are first recognizable by how the stem of the verb differs from the one used in the present system. Perfect stems vary from present stems in at least one of four ways.

1. Syllabic augment: the present stem adds a syllable, usually **-u-**, **-āv-**, or -**īv-**.
   portō becomes **portāvī**
   moneō becomes **monuī**

2. Temporal augment: the vowel of the present stem is lengthened.
   capiō becomes **cēpī**

3. Aorist augment: an **s** is added.
   mittō becomes **mīsī**
   maneō becomes **mansī**

4. Reduplication: repetition of the first syllable or consonant
   currō becomes **cucurrī**

Note: With reduplication, if there is a prefix on the verb, the prefix replaces the reduplication.
   recurrō becomes **recurrī**

Perfect tense

The perfect tense shows a single completed act. For example, **mīsī** can be translated "I sent," "I did send," or "I have sent." The emphasis remains on its having been a single act completed in past time. It also has its own unique set of personal endings, which are attached to the stem formed from the third principal part. They are the same for all verbs, regardless of conjugation, even if the verb is irregular.

mittō, mittere, mīsī, missum, **to send**

mīsī	I sent
mīs**istī**	you sent
mīs**it**	he sent
mīs**imus**	we sent
mīs**istis**	you sent
mīs**ērunt**	they sent

Pluperfect tense

The pluperfect tense shows an action that was completed before some other action in the past. In the English example "The train had left before they reached the station," the train left first, and then they reached the station.

The pluperfect tense employs the same perfect stem from the third principal part as did the perfect. The endings, however, are different.

mittō, mittere, mīsī, missum, **to send**

mīs**eram**	I had sent
mīs**erās**	you had sent
mīs**erat**	he had sent
mīs**erāmus**	we had sent
mīs**erātis**	you had sent
mīs**erant**	they had sent

Future perfect tense

The future perfect tense also shows something happening before something else, except in the future before something else in the future. The strict English version of the future perfect tense includes "will have" with the past participle. In practice, however, English is much less careful than Latin in its representation of this concept, often using the present tense in reference to the future action. In the example "The train will have left before they reach the station," the train will leave first, and then they will reach the station.

Formation of the Latin future perfect begins with the perfect stem, followed by the tense indicator **-eri-** and the usual personal ending. The first person singular contracts the **-i-** with the **-ō**.

mittō, mittere, mīsī, missum, **to send**

mīs**erō**	I will have sent
mīs**eris**	you will have sent
mīs**erit**	he will have sent
mīs**erimus**	we will have sent
mīs**eritis**	you will have sent
mīs**erint**	they will have sent

Exercise 6.1

Conjugate the following verb in the tenses specified: **sūmō, sūmere, sumpsī, sumptum,** to take up.

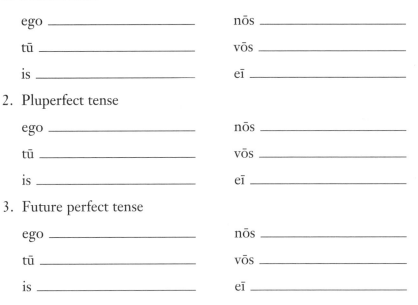

1. Perfect tense

    ego _____   nōs _____

    tū _____   vōs _____

    is _____   eī _____

2. Pluperfect tense

    ego _____   nōs _____

    tū _____   vōs _____

    is _____   eī _____

3. Future perfect tense

    ego _____   nōs _____

    tū _____   vōs _____

    is _____   eī _____

Exercise 6.2

Write the forms of the following verbs in perfect tense in the person and number indicated.

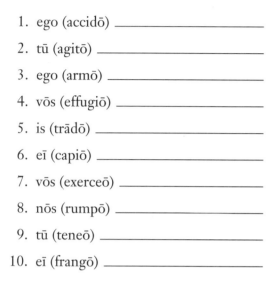

1. ego (accidō) _____

2. tū (agitō) _____

3. ego (armō) _____

4. vōs (effugiō) _____

5. is (trādō) _____

6. eī (capiō) _____

7. vōs (exerceō) _____

8. nōs (rumpō) _____

9. tū (teneō) _____

10. eī (frangō) _____

Exercise 6.3

Write the forms of the following verbs in pluperfect tense in the person and number indicated.

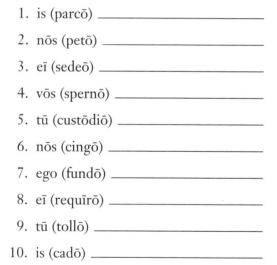

1. is (parcō) _____

2. nōs (petō) _____

3. eī (sedeō) _____

4. vōs (spernō) _____

5. tū (custōdiō) _____

6. nōs (cingō) _____

7. ego (fundō) _____

8. eī (requīrō) _____

9. tū (tollō) _____

10. is (cadō) _____

Exercise 6.4

Write the forms of the following verbs in future perfect tense in the person and number indicated.

1. vōs (inveniō) _____

2. is (portō) _____

3. tū (premō) _____

4. is (serviō) _____

5. eī (veniō) _____

6. nōs (recipiō) _____

7. eī (alō) _____

8. ego (caedō) _____

9. nōs (tendō) _____

10. vōs (audiō) _____

Exercise 6.5

Translate the following verbs into English.

1. cōgitāvī _____

2. crēdidit _____

3. placuerint _____

4. posuerō _____

5. coēgit _____

6. contenderāmus _____

7. vigilāvistis _____

8. fefellerat _____

9. iūrāvit _____

10. invīderam _____

11. reppererimus _____

12. vocāvērunt _____

13. iūvērunt _____

14. nuntiāverant _____

15. patuistis _____

16. incēperit _____

17. texistis _____

18. ēripuistī _____

19. miscuī _____

20. vīcimus _____

Exercise 6.6

Translate the following verbs into Latin using the vocabulary provided.

1. you (pl.) will have spread (**sternō**) _____

2. you (sing.) had worked (**laborō**) _____

3. they had changed (**mutō**) _____

4. you (sing.) thought (**existimō**) _____

5. they told (**narrō**) _____

6. I opened (**pandō**) _____

7. we had done nothing (**cessō**) _____

8. he had finished (**conficiō**) _____

9. he ran (**currō**) _____

10. you (pl.) had set up (**instituō**) _____

11. I had been strong (**valeō**) _____

12. it will have carried (**vehō**) _____

13. I will have called (**appellō**) _____

14. you (pl.) joined (**iungō**) _____

15. they will have offered (**praebeō**) _____

7

Passive Voice
Present System

"Voice" is the grammatical term used to describe the relationship between a subject and a verb. In active voice the subject performs the action of a verb; in passive voice the subject receives the action.

active voice	Caesar hostēs vincet	Caesar will conquer the enemy.
passive voice	hostēs (ā Caesare) vincentur	The enemy will be conquered (by Caesar).

In Latin, passive voice is shown in the present system tenses (i.e. present, imperfect, and future) by means of a special set of personal endings.

active voice	*passive voice*
-ō/-m	-r/-or
-s	-ris
-t	-tur
-mus	-mur
-tis	-minī
-nt	-ntur

Present tense conjugation in passive voice varies across the conjugations and uses the special passive personal endings in place of active ones. The exception lies in the second person singular of third and third **-iō** conjugation verbs where the expected stem vowel **i** becomes **e**.

port**or**	mon**eor**	mitt**or**	cap**ior**	sent**ior**
port**āris**	mon**ēris**	mitt**eris**	cap**eris**	sent**īris**
port**atur**	mon**ētur**	mitt**itur**	cap**itur**	sent**ītur**
port**āmur**	mon**ēmur**	mitt**imur**	cap**imur**	sent**īmur**
port**āminī**	mon**ēminī**	mitt**iminī**	cap**iminī**	sent**īminī**
port**antur**	mon**entur**	mitt**untur**	cap**iuntur**	sent**iuntur**

Imperfect tense conjugation in passive voice substitutes passive for active endings, e.g., port**ā**bar, portā**bāris**, portā**bātur**, etc.

Future tense conjugation in passive voice also shows the same substitution across the conjugations, but with one exception. The second person singular ending for first and second conjugation verbs is **-beris**.

portābor	monēbor	mittar	capiar	sentiar
portāberis	monēberis	mittēris	capiēris	sentiēris
portābitur	monēbitur	mittētur	capiētur	sentiētur
portābimur	monēbimur	mittēmur	capiēmur	sentiēmur
portābiminī	monēbiminī	mittēminī	capiēminī	sentiēminī
portabuntur	monēbuntur	mittēntur	capientur	sentientur

Exercise 7.1

Conjugate the following verbs in present tense, passive voice.

1. **optō, optāre, optāvī, optātum**, to choose

   ego _____   nōs _____

   tū _____   vōs _____

   is _____   eī _____

2. **caveō, cavēre, cāvī, cautum**, to beware

   ego _____   nōs _____

   tū _____   vōs _____

   is _____   eī _____

3. **contemnō, contemnere, contempsī, contemptum**, to despise

   ego _____   nōs _____

   tū _____   vōs _____

   is _____   eī _____

4. **excipiō, excipere, excēpī, exceptum**, to receive

   ego _____   nōs _____

   tū _____   vōs _____

   is _____   eī _____

Exercise 7.2

Conjugate the following verbs in imperfect tense, passive voice.

1. **induō, induere, induī, indutum**, to dress

    ego _____   nōs _____

    tū _____   vōs _____

    is _____   eī _____

2. **lavō, lavāre, lāvī, lautum**, to wash

    ego _____   nōs _____

    tū _____   vōs _____

    is _____   eī _____

3. **respiciō, respicere, respexī, respectum**, to look back

    ego _____   nōs _____

    tū _____   vōs _____

    is _____   eī _____

Exercise 7.3

Conjugate the following verbs in future tense, passive voice.

1. **sustineō, sustinēre, sustinuī, sustentum**, to uphold

    ego _____   nōs _____

    tū _____   vōs _____

    is _____   eī _____

2. **tangō, tangere, tetigī, tactum**, to touch

    ego _____   nōs _____

    tū _____   vōs _____

    is _____   eī _____

3. **fīniō, fīnīre, fīnīvī, fīnītum**, to finish

    ego _____   nōs _____

    tū _____   vōs _____

    is _____   eī _____

Exercise 7.4

Write the forms of the following verbs in the present passive in the person and number indicated.

1. is (parcō) _____
2. nōs (petō) _____
3. eī (iubeō) _____
4. vōs (spernō) _____
5. tū (custōdiō) _____
6. nōs (cingō) _____
7. ego (relinquō) _____
8. eī (requīrō) _____
9. tū (tollō) _____
10. is (cupiō) _____

Exercise 7.5

Write the forms of the following verbs in the imperfect passive in the person and number indicated.

1. ego (pōnō) _____
2. tū (agitō) _____
3. ego (amō) _____
4. vōs (mūniō) _____
5. is (trādō) _____
6. eī (capiō) _____
7. vōs (exerceō) _____
8. nōs (rumpō) _____
9. tū (teneō) _____
10. eī (frangō) _____

Exercise 7.6

Write the forms of the following verbs in the future passive in the person and number indicated.

1. vōs (inveniō) _____
2. is (portō) _____

3. tū (premō) _____

4. is (iaciō) _____

5. eī (sepeliō) _____

6. nōs (recipiō) _____

7. eī (moneō) _____

8. ego (caedō) _____

9. nōs (tendō) _____

10. vōs (audiō) _____

Exercise 7.7

Translate the following verbs into English.

1. regnābar _____

2. comparābuntur _____

3. intrābatur _____

4. mittēminī _____

5. movētur _____

6. conditur _____

7. mūnīmur _____

8. sepeliēntur _____

9. clauditur _____

10. dūcēris _____

11. dūceris _____

12. permittor _____

13. scrībēbantur _____

14. superātur _____

15. committēbāris _____

16. iacimur _____

17. percutiētur _____

18. implēbitur _____

19. laudāberis _____

20. perdimur _____

Exercise 7.8

Translate the following verbs into Latin using the vocabulary provided.

1. you (pl.) were being deceived (**lūdō**) _____

2. he is being entrusted (**mandō**) _____

3. you (sing.) will be killed (**necō**) _____

4. I will be chosen (**legō**) _____

5. they are being untied (**solvō**) _____

6. we were being consulted (**consūlō**) _____

7. he will be added (**addō**) _____

8. you (sing.) are loved (**dīligō**) _____

9. I am being defended (**defendō**) _____

10. you (pl.) will be taken care of (**cūrō**) _____

8

Passive Voice
Perfect System

There are no special forms for passive voice for the perfect system tenses (i.e., perfect, pluperfect, and future perfect). Instead, Latin uses a combination of the perfect passive participle and present, imperfect, and future tenses of the verb **sum**, **esse**, **fuī**, **futūrus**, respectively.

perfect	*pluperfect*	*future perfect*
missus sum	missus eram	missus erō
missus es	missus erās	missus eris
missus est	missus erat	missus erit
missī sumus	missī erāmus	missī erimus
missī estis	missī erātis	missī eritis
missī sunt	missī erant	missī erunt

It is extremely important to note that these forms include participles, and that the participle must agree in gender and number with the subject of the form of the verb *sum* that is used, whether the subject is expressed or implied. Therefore:

masculine	miss**us** est	**he** was sent	missī sunt	**they** were sent
feminine	miss**a** est	**she** was sent	missae sunt	**they** were sent
neuter	miss**um** est	**it** was sent	missa sunt	**they** were sent

Exercise 8.1

Conjugate the following verbs in perfect tense, passive voice, masculine gender.

1. **debeō, debēre, debuī, debitum,** to owe

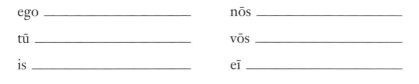

2. **faciō, facere, fēcī, factum**, to do

    ego _____   nōs _____

    tū _____   vōs _____

    is _____   eī _____

Exercise 8.2

Conjugate the following verbs in perfect tense, passive voice, feminine gender.

1. **emō, emere, ēmī, emptum**, to buy

    ego _____   nōs _____

    tū _____   vōs _____

    ea _____   eae _____

2. **gerō, gerere, gessī, gestum**, to carry, accomplish, wear (clothes)

    ego _____   nōs _____

    tū _____   vōs _____

    ea _____   eae _____

Exercise 8.3

Conjugate the following verbs in pluperfect tense, passive voice, masculine gender.

1. **noscō, noscere, nōvī, nōtum**, to learn, know

    ego _____   nōs _____

    tū _____   vōs _____

    is _____   eī _____

2. **aperiō, aperīre, aperuī, apertum**, to open

    ego _____   nōs _____

    tū _____   vōs _____

    is _____   eī _____

Exercise 8.4

Conjugate the following verbs in pluperfect tense, passive voice, neuter gender.

1. **ostendō, ostendere, ostendī, ostentum**, to show

   ego _____   nōs _____

   tū _____   vōs _____

   id _____   ea _____

2. **colligō, colligere, collēgī, collectum**, to gather

   ego _____   nōs _____

   tū _____   vōs _____

   id _____   ea _____

Exercise 8.5

Conjugate the following verbs in future perfect tense, passive voice, masculine gender.

1. **sinō, sinere, sīvī, situm**, to let, allow

   ego _____   nōs _____

   tū _____   vōs _____

   is _____   eī _____

2. **retineō, retinēre, retinuī, retentum**, to hold back

   ego _____   nōs _____

   tū _____   vōs _____

   is _____   eī _____

Exercise 8.6

Write the forms of the following verbs in the perfect passive, masculine gender, in the person and number indicated.

1. vōs (caedō) _____

2. tū (petō) _____

3. eī (dīvidō) _____

4. tū (spernō) _____

5. vōs (custōdiō) _____

6. nōs (legō) _____

7. is (laudō) _____

8. eī (occupō) _____

9. is (tollō) _____

10. eī (recipiō) _____

Exercise 8.7

Write the forms of the following verbs in the pluperfect passive, feminine gender, in the person and number indicated.

1. ego (pōnō) _____

2. tū (līberō) _____

3. eae (faciō) _____

4. vōs (trādō) _____

5. ea (trādō) _____

6. eae (iaciō) _____

7. ego (spernō) _____

8. nōs (vincō) _____

9. tū (augeō) _____

10. ea (rumpō) _____

Exercise 8.8

Write the forms of the following verbs in the future perfect passive, masculine gender, in the person and number indicated.

1. is (inveniō) _____

2. vōs (portō) _____

3. tū (premō) _____

4. vōs (iaciō) _____

5. eī (sepeliō) _____

6. nōs (recipiō) _____

7. eī (moneō) _____

8. nōs (caedō) _____

9. ego (tendō) _____

10. is (audiō) _____

Exercise 8.9

Translate the following verbs into English.

1. victī erāmus _____

2. dīlectus es _____

3. exercitus eris _____

4. bibitum erat _____

5. captus sum _____

6. iūtī erimus _____

7. audīta erat _____

8. mutāta sunt _____

9. creātī erunt _____

10. indūtus est _____

11. pulsī erant _____

12. sublātum est _____

13. occīsus eris _____

14. intellectus eram _____

15. laesa est _____

16. auctī eritis _____

17. portāta erant _____

18. ruptum est _____

19. scissī erunt _____

20. additus erō _____

Exercise 8.10

Translate the following verbs into Latin using the vocabulary provided.

1. I was seen (**videō**) _____

2. you (pl.) will have been heard (**audiō**) _____

3. it has been added (**addō**) _____

4. she was denied (**negō**) _____

5. it had not been known (**nesciō**) _____

6. I had been deceived (**fallō**) _____

7. they will have been finished (**fīniō**) _____

8. you (pl.) were led (**dūcō**) _____

9. you (sing.) were called back (**revocō**) _____

10. we will have been welcomed (**accipiō**) _____

9

Deponent Verbs

There is a special group of verbs called "deponents" that appear to have only passive forms, but have only active meanings.

Middle voice

The reason for this apparent contradiction is that in addition to active voice, where the subject performs the action of a verb, and passive voice, where the subject receives it, there is "middle voice." In middle voice the subject performs the action upon itself, has a strong interest in the action, or is otherwise personally connected with the action.

Deponent verbs

While almost any verb can take middle voice, it is most commonly seen in these verbs, which have *only* middle voice forms and meaning. What makes deponents challenging is that middle voice forms are identical to passive voice forms and their meanings sound active.

Deponent verbs are easily recognized by their principal parts. Having no active forms (except for present and future participles), passive form equivalents are substituted.

first conjugation	conor, conārī, conātus sum
second conjugation	vereor, verērī, veritus sum
third conjugation	nascor, nascī, nātus sum
third conjugation -iō	patior, patī, passus sum
fourth conjugation	orior, orīrī, ortus sum

Semideponent verbs

There is a small group of verbs called semideponents, which, as their name suggests, are only half deponent. Their present system is regular, and only their perfect system is deponent. These verbs are also recognizable by their principal parts, e.g., **audeō, audēre, ausus sum**.

common deponent and semideponent verbs
first conjugation
arbitror, arbitrārī, arbitrātus sum, to think
conor, conārī, conātus sum, to try, attempt
cunctor, cunctārī, cunctātus sum, to hesitate, delay
hortor, hortārī, hortātus sum, to encourage, urge
imitor, imitārī, imitātus sum, to copy
mīror, mīrārī, mīrātus sum, to marvel at, wonder, be amazed
moror, morārī, morātus sum, to hesitate, delay, kill time
precor, precārī, precātus sum, to pray

second conjugation
audeō, audēre, ausus sum, to dare
confiteor, confitērī, confessus sum, to confess, admit
gaudeō, gaudēre, gāvīsus sum, to rejoice, be happy
polliceor, pollicērī, pollicitus sum, to promise
reor, rērī, ratus sum, to think, judge
tueor, tuērī, tūtus sum, to watch, protect
vereor, verērī, veritus sum, to be afraid

third conjugation
complector, complectī, complexus sum, to hug, embrace
consequor, consequī, consecūtus sum, to follow, pursue, obtain
fruor, fruī, fructus sum, to enjoy (usually with ablative)
fungor, fungī, functus sum, to perform (usually with ablative)
irascor, irascī, irātus sum, to become angry
lābor, lābī, lapsus sum, to slip
loquor, loquī, locūtus sum, to talk, speak
nascor, nascī, nātus sum, to be born
oblīvīscor, oblīvīscī, oblītus sum, to forget (with genitive)
proficiscor, proficiscī, profectus sum, to set out, leave
queror, querī, questus sum, to complain
sequor, sequī, secūtus sum, to follow

ulciscor, ulciscī, ultus sum, to avenge

ūtor, ūtī, ūsus sum (with ablative), to use; to benefit oneself (by means of)

third conjugation -iō

aggredior, aggredī, aggressus sum, to approach, attack

ēgredior, ēgredī, ēgressus sum, to leave, go out

ingredior, ingredī, ingressus sum, to step in, begin

morior, morī, mortuus sum (fut. part. moritūrus), to die

patior, patī, passus sum, to suffer, experience

fourth conjugation

experior, experīrī, expertus sum, to try, test, prove

mentior, mentīrī, mentītus sum, to lie, deceive

orior, orīrī, ortus sum, to rise

potior, potīrī, potītus sum, to acquire

Exercise 9.1

Conjugate the following deponents in present tense.

1. **lābor, lābī, lapsus sum**, to slip

ego _____   nōs _____

tū _____   vōs _____

is _____   eī _____

2. **precor, precārī, precātus sum**, to pray, beg

ego _____   nōs _____

tū _____   vōs _____

is _____   eī _____

Exercise 9.2

Conjugate the following deponents in perfect tense, feminine gender.

1. **audeō, audēre, ausus sum**, to dare

ego _____   nōs _____

tū _____   vōs _____

ea _____   eae _____

2. **experior, experīrī, expertus sum**, to try

ego _____	nōs _____
tū _____	vōs _____
ea _____	eae _____

Exercise 9.3

Conjugate the following deponents in pluperfect tense, neuter gender.

1. **ulciscor, ulciscī, ultus sum**, to avenge

ego _____	nōs _____
tū _____	vōs _____
id _____	ea _____

2. **cunctor, cunctārī, cunctātus sum**, to hesitate

ego _____	nōs _____
tū _____	vōs _____
id _____	ea _____

Exercise 9.4

Conjugate the following deponents in future tense.

1. **patior, patī, passus sum**, to suffer

ego _____	nōs _____
tū _____	vōs _____
is _____	eī _____

2. **tueor, tuērī, tūtus sum**, to protect

ego _____	nōs _____
tū _____	vōs _____
is _____	eī _____

Exercise 9.5

Write the forms of the following deponents in perfect tense, masculine gender, in the person and number indicated.

1. vōs (moror) _____
2. tū (sequor) _____
3. eī (cunctor) _____
4. tū (morior) _____
5. ego (queror) _____
6. nōs (fungor) _____
7. is (conor) _____
8. eī (ūtor) _____
9. is (imitor) _____
10. nōs (fruor) _____

Exercise 9.6

Write the forms of the following deponents in present tense in the person and number indicated.

1. ego (mīror) _____
2. tū (arbitror) _____
3. eī (potior) _____
4. vōs (patior) _____
5. is (experior) _____
6. eī (orior) _____
7. ego (hortor) _____
8. nōs (consequor) _____
9. tū (irascor) _____
10. is (tueor) _____

Exercise 9.7

Write the forms of the following deponents in pluperfect tense, feminine gender, in the person and number indicated.

1. ea (proficīscor) _____
2. vōs (ēgredior) _____
3. tū (ingredior) _____
4. ego (nascor) _____
5. eae (aggredior) _____
6. nōs (loquor) _____
7. eae (polliceor) _____
8. nōs (confiteor) _____
9. ego (oblīvīscor) _____
10. ea (gaudeō) _____

Exercise 9.8

Write the forms of the following deponents in imperfect tense in the person and number indicated.

1. tū (reor) _____
2. is (mentior) _____
3. eī (vereor) _____
4. nōs (lābor) _____
5. ego (ulciscor) _____
6. eī (precor) _____
7. ego (complector) _____
8. vōs (moror) _____
9. is (ūtor) _____
10. is (mīror) _____

Exercise 9.9

Translate the following verbs into English.

1. ēgressa erat _____
2. functī eritis _____
3. passae erant _____
4. morātur _____
5. nātus sum _____
6. oblītī erimus _____
7. confitēbantur _____
8. aggrediēbāminī _____
9. morientur _____
10. potiētur _____
11. secūta erat _____
12. ulciscuntur _____
13. rēbāris _____
14. arbitrāberis _____
15. ūsa es _____
16. ingressus erit _____
17. complectitur _____
18. mīrāris _____
19. consequēbar _____
20. gāvīsa est _____

Exercise 9.10

Translate the following verbs into Latin using the vocabulary provided.

1. we are trying (**experior**) _____
2. I had set out (**proficiscor**) _____
3. we prayed (**precor**) _____
4. you (sing.) were trying (**conor**) _____

5. I am afraid (**vereor**) _____

6. they had spoken (**loquor**) _____

7. you (pl.) will hesitate (**cunctor**) _____

8. he was dying (**morior**) _____

9. she will protect (**tueor**) _____

10. he was urging (**hortor**) _____

10

Participles and Gerunds

Participles

Participles are verbal adjectives. As verb forms they have tense and voice; as adjectives they must be able to agree in case, number, and gender with nouns.

Latin has four participles: present active, perfect passive, future active, and future passive, which is often equated with the gerundive.

first conjugation

	active	*passive*
present	portans, -ntis	—
perfect	—	portātus, -a, -um
future	portātūrus, -a, -um	portandus, -a, -um

second conjugation

	active	*passive*
present	monens, -ntis	—
perfect	—	monitus, -a, -um
future	monitūrus, -a, -um	monendus, -a, -um

third conjugation

	active	*passive*
present	mittens, -ntis	—
perfect	—	missus, -a, -um
future	missūrus, -a, -um	mittendus, -a, -um

third conjugation -*iō*

	active	*passive*
present	capiens, -ntis	—
perfect	—	captus, -a, -um
future	captūrus, -a, -um	capiendus, -a, -um

fourth conjugation

	active	*passive*
present	sentiens, -ntis	—
perfect	—	sensus, -a, -um
future	sensūrus, -a, -um	sentiendus, -a, -um

The present active participle is formed with the present system stem plus **-ens, -entis**. It is declined as a third declension adjective of one termination (cf. the adjective **ingens, ingentis**). Its tense value is concurrent with that of the main verb, for example, **capiens** ("taking").

The future passive participle (gerundive) is also formed with the present system stem. It is a first/second declension adjective (cf. **bonus, -a, -um**). Taken as a participle, it refers to an action about to be completed after that of the main verb, for example, **capiendus** ("about to be taken"). Taken as a gerundive, it denotes necessity or obligation, for example, **capiendus** ("must or ought to be taken").

The perfect passive participle is a first/second declension adjective and is often used as the fourth principal part of a verb. It can be recognized by its ending in **-tus** or **-sus**. This book follows another tradition for listing principal parts, which uses instead the supine, ending in **-tum** or **-sum**. The tense value of the perfect passive participle shows an action that has already occurred before that of the main verb, for example, **fractus** ("broken").

The future active participle is a first/second declension adjective formed by adding **-ūrus** to the stem provided by the perfect passive participle. It refers to an action that is going to happen after the main verb or intent, for example, **captūrus** ("about to take").

Gerunds

The gerund is a noun made from a verb. It is neuter singular and has no nominative form, nor is there a plural. The gerund in English sounds like the present participle, as in **monendī** ("of warning"), **monendō** ("to/for warning"), etc., but it must be remembered that it is a noun.

nominative	—	—	—	—	—
genitive	portandī	monendī	mittendī	capiendī	sentiendī

dative	portandō	monendō	mittendō	capiendō	sentiendō
accusative	portandum	monendum	mittendum	capiendum	sentiendum
ablative	portandō	monendī	mittendō	capiendō	sentiendō

Exercise 10.1

Complete the following participle charts for the verbs provided.

1. **aperiō, aperīre, aperuī, apertum,** to open

	active	passive
present	_____	_____
perfect	_____	_____
future	_____	_____

2. **augeō, augēre, auxī, auctum,** to increase

	active	passive
present	_____	_____
perfect	_____	_____
future	_____	_____

3. **indicō, indicāre, indicāvī, indicātum,** to make known

	active	passive
present	_____	_____
perfect	_____	_____
future	_____	_____

4. **iaciō, iacere, iēcī, iactum,** to throw

	active	passive
present	_____	_____
perfect	_____	_____
future	_____	_____

5. **constituō, constituere, constituī, constitūtum,** to stand something up

	active	passive
present	_____	_____
perfect	_____	_____
future	_____	_____

Exercise 10.2

Complete the following gerund charts for the verbs provided.

1. **regnō**, **regnāre**, **regnāvī**, **regnātum**, to rule

nominative _____

genitive _____

dative _____

accusative _____

ablative _____

2. **ardeō**, **ardēre**, **arsī**, **arsum**, to burn

nominative _____

genitive _____

dative _____

accusative _____

ablative _____

3. **parcō**, **parcere**, **pepercī**, **parsum**, to spare

nominative _____

genitive _____

dative _____

accusative _____

ablative _____

4. **capiō**, **capere**, **cēpī**, **captum**, to take

nominative _____

genitive _____

dative _____

accusative _____

ablative _____

5. **inveniō**, **invenīre**, **invēnī**, **inventum**, to find

nominative _____

genitive _____

dative _____

accusative _____

ablative _____

Exercise 10.3

Translate the following participles into English.

1. gaudēns _____

2. ambulandus _____

3. certandus _____

4. dubitātūrus _____

5. memorandus _____

6. parsūrus _____

7. superātus _____

8. cursūrus _____

9. parātūrus _____

10. perficiens _____

11. ōrans _____

12. confitendus _____

13. mixtūrus _____

14. vetitus _____

15. incipiendus _____

16. surgens _____

17. merendus _____

18. metūtus _____

19. sparsus _____

20. fingens _____

Exercise 10.4

Translate the following participles into Latin using the vocabulary provided.

1. holding (**teneō**) _____

2. ought (**petō**) _____

3. must be fought (**pugnō**) _____

4. called back (**revocō**) _____

5. despising (**contemnō**) _____

6. about to teach (**doceō**) _____

7. living (**vīvō**) _____

8. must be carried (**ferō**) _____

9. kept (**retineō**) _____

10. about to weep (**fleō**) _____

11

Imperative Mood

Commands in Latin are expressed by imperative mood. Imperative mood is extremely easy to form and recognize. Active forms for all conjugations are as follows. The singular form is used to issue a command to one person, the plural to more than one.

	singular	*plural*	
first conjugation	portā!	portāte!	carry!
second conjugation	monē!	monēte!	advise!
third conjugation	mitte!	mittite!	send!
third conjugation -iō	cape!	capite!	take!
fourth conjugation	sentī!	sentīte!	feel!

Note: There are four common verbs with irregular imperative forms:

	singular	*plural*	
dicō, dicere	dīc!	dīcite!	speak!
ducō, ducere	dūc!	dūcite!	lead!
faciō, facere	fac!	facite!	do!
ferō, ferre	fer!	ferte!	carry!

Passive imperative forms, as used by deponent verbs, are different.

	singular	*plural*	
first conjugation	conāre!	conāminī!	try!
second conjugation	verēre!	verēminī!	be afraid!
third conjugation	sequere!	sequiminī!	follow!
third conjugation -iō	patere!	patiminī!	endure!
fourth conjugation	orīre!	orīminī!	arise!

Negative commands are formed quite differently. They use the words **nolī** and **nolīte** with the infinitive, regardless of conjugation. For example:

	singular	*plural*	
nolī portāre!	nolīte portāre!	don't carry!	

Exercise 11.1

Put the following verbs in imperative mood.

1. **pāreō, pārēre, pāruī, pāritum**, to obey

	singular	plural
positive	_____	_____
negative	_____	_____

2. **caedō, caedere, cecīdī, caesum**, to cut

	singular	plural
positive	_____	_____
negative	_____	_____

3. **sciō, scīre, scīvī, scītum**, to know

	singular	plural
positive	_____	_____
negative	_____	_____

4. **recipiō, recipere, recēpī, receptum**, to accept

	singular	plural
positive	_____	_____
negative	_____	_____

5. **negō, negāre, negāvī, negātum**, to deny

	singular	plural
positive	_____	_____
negative	_____	_____

6. **faciō, facere, fēcī, factum**, to make, do

	singular	plural
positive	_____	_____
negative	_____	_____

7. **ferō, ferre, tulī, lātum**, to bring

	singular	plural
positive	_____	_____
negative	_____	_____

8. **audeō, audēre, ausus sum**, to dare

	singular	plural
positive	_____	_____
negative	_____	_____

9. **vereor, verērī, veritus sum**, to be afraid

	singular	plural
positive	_____	_____
negative	_____	_____

10. **conor, conārī, conātus sum**, to try

	singular	plural
positive	_____	_____
negative	_____	_____

Exercise 11.2

Translate the following commands into English.

1. conde! _____

2. recipe! _____

3. sternite! _____

4. dēlēte! _____

5. nolīte iacēre! _____

6. sequere! _____

7. ingrediminī! _____

8. nolī conārī! _____

9. nolīte dūcere! _____

10. cōgitā! _____

Exercise 11.3

Translate the following commands into Latin using the vocabulary provided.

1. Seize! (pl.) (**occupō**) _____

2. Don't get dressed! (pl.) (**induō**) _____

3. Arrive! (sing.) (**perveniō**) _____

4. Don't get angry! (sing.) (**irascor**) _____

5. Untie! (sing.) (**solvō**) _____

12

Infinitives

The infinitive is a verb form that has both tense and voice and refers to an action in general terms.

first conjugation

	active	*passive*
present	portāre (to carry)	portārī (to be carried)
perfect	portāvisse (to have carried)	portātus esse (to have been carried)
future	portātūrus esse	portātum īrī
	(to be about to carry)	(to be about to be carried)

second conjugation

	active	*passive*
present	monēre	monērī
perfect	monuisse	monitus esse
future	monitūrus esse	monitum īrī

third conjugation

	active	*passive*
present	mittere	mittī
perfect	mīsisse	missus esse
future	missūrus esse	missum īrī

third conjugation *-iō*

	active	*passive*
present	capere	capī
perfect	cēpisse	captus esse
future	captūrus esse	captum īrī

fourth conjugation

	active	*passive*
present	sentīre	sentīrī
perfect	sensisse	sensus esse
future	sensūrus esse	sensum īrī

The second principal part of a verb is the present infinitive active. It varies in formation across the conjugations. For deponents, it is the present infinitive passive. The present infinitive is also the criterion by which verbs are sorted into conjugations.

Formation of perfect and future infinitives is the same for all verbs, regardless of conjugation.

The perfect infinitive active is formed from the perfect active stem with the ending **-isse**.

The perfect infinitive passive is a compound construction using the perfect passive participle with the present infinitive of the verb **sum**.

The future infinitive active is also a compound construction. It uses the future active participle with the present infinitive of the verb **sum**.

The future infinitive passive is another compound construction formed with the supine and **īrī**, which is the present infinitive passive of the verb **eō, īre**.

Exercise 12.1

Complete the following infinitive charts for the verbs provided.

1. **perdō, perdere, perdidī, perditum,** to lose

	active	passive
present	_____	_____
perfect	_____	_____
future	_____	_____

2. **inveniō, invenīre, invēnī, inventum,** to find

	active	passive
present	_____	_____
perfect	_____	_____
future	_____	_____

3. **moneō, monēre, monuī, monitum**, to warn

	active	passive
present	_____	_____
perfect	_____	_____
future	_____	_____

4. **pariō, parere, peperī, partum**, to give birth, produce

	active	passive
present	_____	_____
perfect	_____	_____
future	_____	_____

5. **armō, armāre, armāvī, armātum**, to arm

	active	passive
present	_____	_____
perfect	_____	_____
future	_____	_____

Exercise 12.2

Translate the following infinitives into English.

1. genuisse _____
2. ignōrārī _____
3. lectus esse _____
4. aggredī _____
5. armātum īrī _____
6. mansisse _____
7. studēre _____
8. sumptūrus esse _____
9. volātūrus esse _____
10. lavārī _____
11. vīcisse _____
12. commīsisse _____
13. crēdī _____

14. iuvārī _____

15. scissum īrī _____

16. accēpisse _____

17. dīlexisse _____

18. necāre _____

19. occīsus esse _____

20. pulsus esse _____

Exercise 12.3

Translate the following verbs into Latin using the vocabulary provided.

1. to be about to drink (**bibō**) _____

2. to have set out (**proficiscor**) _____

3. to hurry (**properō**) _____

4. to be afraid (**timeō**) _____

5. to be elected (**creō**) _____

6. to have been hit (**percutiō**) _____

7. to pray (**precor**) _____

8. to have thought (**reor**) _____

9. to be about to be said (**dīcō**) _____

10. to be about to fill (**impleō**) _____

13

Subjunctive Mood

Present and Perfect Tenses

The grammatical term "mood" refers to the way a speaker treats an action. The indicative mood treats an action as fact, the imperative mood expresses a command, and the subjunctive mood views an action as a wish or idea.

Latin uses the subjunctive mood in a host of different constructions for which English uses very different approaches. There is no single way to translate a Latin verb in subjunctive mood into English. For this reason, and for the sake of simplicity, this book translates subjunctive mood forms the same as their indicative mood counterparts.

Present subjunctive

As is true for the present indicative, forms of the present subjunctive vary across the conjugations. The most noticeable variation between the moods is in the theme vowel. The dominant stem vowel in first conjugation is **-a-**. To mark the subjunctive, that vowel switches to **-e-**. The other conjugations adopt an **-a-**.

A good way to remember present subjunctive formation is to go to the first principal part of a verb, and for first conjugation change the final **-o** to **-e-** and then apply either active or passive personal endings. For all the other conjugations change the final **-o** to **-a-**, and apply either active or passive personal endings. The following chart illustrates only the active voice forms. For the passive, simply exchange -**m** with -**r**, -**s** with -**ris**, and so on.

portem	moneam	mittam	capiam	sentiam
portēs	moneās	mittās	capiās	sentiās
portet	moneat	mittat	capiat	sentiat
portēmus	moneāmus	mittāmus	capiāmus	sentiāmus
portētis	moneātis	mittātis	capiātis	sentiātis
portent	moneant	mittant	capiant	sentiant

Perfect subjunctive

The perfect subjunctive is perhaps the least common verb form. The active forms are almost identical to the future perfect indicative, varying only in the first person singular. The passive forms are compound; that is, they are made with the perfect passive participle and the present subjunctive of the verb **sum** as in this example with the verb **mitto**.

active	*passive*
mīserim	missus sim
mīseris	missus sīs
mīserit	missus sit
mīserimus	missī sīmus
mīseritis	missī sītis
mīserint	missī sint

Exercise 13.1

Conjugate the following verbs in present subjunctive active.

1. **neglegō, neglegere, neglexī, neglectum,** to neglect

   ego _____   nōs _____

   tū _____   vōs _____

   is _____   eī _____

2. **amō, amāre, amāvī, amātum,** to love

   ego _____   nōs _____

   tū _____   vōs _____

   is _____   eī _____

3. **fugiō, fugere, fūgī, fugitum,** to run away

   ego _____   nōs _____

   tū _____   vōs _____

   is _____   eī _____

4. **videō, vidēre, vīdī, vīsum,** to see

   ego _____   nōs _____

   tū _____   vōs _____

   is _____   eī _____

Exercise 13.2

Conjugate the following verbs in the present subjunctive passive.

1. **laedō, laedere, laesī, laesum**, to hurt

   ego _____   nōs _____

   tū _____   vōs _____

   is _____   eī _____

2. **spectō, spectāre, spectāvī, spectātum**, to watch

   ego _____   nōs _____

   tū _____   vōs _____

   is _____   eī _____

3. **ulciscor, ulciscī, ultus sum**, to avenge

   ego _____   nōs _____

   tū _____   vōs _____

   is _____   eī _____

4. **mentior, mentīrī, mentītus sum**, to lie

   ego _____   nōs _____

   tū _____   vōs _____

   is _____   eī _____

Exercise 13.3

Conjugate the following verbs in the perfect subjunctive active.

1. **tegō, tegere, texī, tectum**, to cover

   ego _____   nōs _____

   tū _____   vōs _____

   is _____   eī _____

2. **veniō, venīre, vēnī, ventum**, to come

   ego _____   nōs _____

   tū _____   vōs _____

   is _____   eī _____

Exercise 13.4

Conjugate the following verbs in the perfect subjunctive passive.

1. **fundō, fundere, fūdī, fūsum**, to pour

    ego _____   nōs _____

    tū _____   vōs _____

    is _____   eī _____

2. **queror, querī, questus sum**, to complain

    ego _____   nōs _____

    tū _____   vōs _____

    is _____   eī _____

Exercise 13.5

Write the following verbs in the present subjunctive active in the person provided.

1. tū (colligō) _____

2. is (crescō) _____

3. nōs (cēdō) _____

4. eī (trādō) _____

5. eī (existimō) _____

6. ego (relinquō) _____

7. eī (āmittō) _____

8. ego (cessō) _____

9. vōs (colō) _____

10. is (exerceō) _____

11. tū (temptō) _____

12. eī (respiciō) _____

13. is (celebrō) _____

14. nōs (fīgō) _____

15. is (sentiō) _____

Exercise 13.6

Write the following verbs in the present subjunctive passive in the person provided.

1. tū (comparō) _____
2. eī (quaerō) _____
3. vōs (queror) _____
4. nōs (reperiō) _____
5. vōs (agitō) _____
6. nōs (aspiciō) _____
7. eī (custōdiō) _____
8. ego (laudō) _____
9. ego (hortor) _____
10. is (sustineō) _____
11. tū (institutō) _____
12. is (reddō) _____
13. is (polliceor) _____
14. is (appellō) _____
15. eī (orior) _____

Exercise 13.7

Write the following verbs in the perfect subjunctive active in the person provided.

1. vōs (mittō) _____
2. is (capiō) _____
3. is (pōnō) _____
4. is (postulō) _____
5. vōs (agō) _____
6. is (pateō) _____
7. nōs (trahō) _____
8. eī (discō) _____
9. ego (gerō) _____
10. nōs (ostendō) _____

Exercise 13.8

Write the following verbs in the perfect subjunctive passive in the person provided.

1. ego (ēgredior) _____
2. vōs (vocō) _____
3. eī (addō) _____
4. is (dō) _____
5. vōs (fallō) _____
6. tū (imitor) _____
7. eī (lūdō) _____
8. is (rapiō) _____
9. ego (moror) _____
10. is (mutō) _____

Exercise 13.9

Translate the following verbs into English.

1. conficiātur _____
2. alātis _____
3. cāverim _____
4. persuadeam _____
5. serviant _____
6. consulāminī _____
7. laborāverimus _____
8. scrībant _____
9. complectar _____
10. caruerit _____
11. dīvīsus sit _____
12. iunctī sint _____
13. cupiās _____
14. nuntiētis _____
15. sepeliantur _____

16. sināmur _____

17. nocueris _____

18. audiāminī _____

19. intendatur _____

20. falsī sint _____

Exercise 13.10

Translate the following verbs into Latin using the vocabulary provided.

1. I am riding (**vehō**) _____

2. you (sing.) are in the habit (**soleō**) _____

3. you (pl.) are trying (**experior**) _____

4. they live (**habitō**) _____

5. we have defended (**dēfendō**) _____

6. they were turned back (**revertō**) _____

7. he is singing (**canō**) _____

8. you (sing.) have been touched (**tangō**) _____

9. she was amazed (**mīror**) _____

10. they have died (**morior**) _____

14

Subjunctive Mood
Imperfect and Pluperfect Tenses

The grammatical term "mood" refers to the way a speaker treats an action. The indicative mood treats an action as fact, the imperative mood expresses a command, and the subjunctive mood views an action as a wish or idea.

Latin uses the subjunctive mood in a host of different constructions for which English uses very different approaches. There is no single way to translate a Latin verb in subjunctive mood into English. For this reason, and for the sake of simplicity, this book translates subjunctive mood forms the same as their indicative mood counterparts.

Imperfect subjunctive

The imperfect subjunctive is easy to recognize. Where the imperfect indicative has **-ba-** as a tense indicator, the imperfect subjunctive has **-re-**.

portārem	monērem	mitterem	caperem	sentīrem
portārēs	monērēs	mitterēs	caperēs	sentīrēs
portāret	monēret	mitteret	caperet	sentīret
portārēmus	monērēmus	mitterēmus	caperēmus	sentīrēmus
portārētis	monērētis	mitterētis	caperētis	sentīrētis
portārent	monērent	mitterent	caperent	sentīrent

Another way to remember its formation is that it appears to have the present infinitive active with the regular active or passive personal endings attached. For deponents, the personal endings appear to be attached to what the present infinitive would have been had there been one. For example, the present infinitive active of the deponent **patior, patī, passus sum** would have been **patere**, so its imperfect subjunctive forms are **paterer, patereris,** etc.

Pluperfect subjunctive

The tense/mood indicator for the pluperfect subjunctive active is **-isse-**. Another way to remember and recognize it is by seeing it as the perfect infinitive active with a personal ending. The passive forms are compound: that is, they are formed with the perfect passive participle and the imperfect subjunctive of the verb **sum**. Here too the forms can be seen as the perfect passive infinitive with personal endings.

active	*passive*
mīsissem	missus essem
mīsissēs	missus essēs
mīsisset	missus esset
mīsissēmus	missī essēmus
mīsissētis	missī essētis
mīsissent	missī essent

Exercise 14.1

Conjugate the following verbs in the imperfect subjunctive active.

1. **cernō, cernere, crēvī, crētum**, to distinguish

    ego _____   nōs _____

    tū _____   vōs _____

    is _____   eī _____

2. **narrō, narrāre, narrāvī, narrātum**, to tell

    ego _____   nōs _____

    tū _____   vōs _____

    is _____   eī _____

Exercise 14.2

Conjugate the following verbs in the imperfect subjunctive passive.

1. **fruor, fruī, frūctus sum**, to enjoy

    ego _____   nōs _____

    tū _____   vōs _____

    is _____   eī _____

2. **fīniō, fīnīre, fīnīvī, fīnītum**, to finish

ego _____   nōs _____

tū _____   vōs _____

is _____   eī _____

Exercise 14.3

Conjugate the following verbs in the pluperfect subjunctive active.

1. **lateō, latēre, latuī**, to lie hidden

ego _____   nōs _____

tū _____   vōs _____

is _____   eī _____

2. **intrō, intrāre, intrāvī, intrātum**, to enter

ego _____   nōs _____

tū _____   vōs _____

is _____   eī _____

Exercise 14.4

Conjugate the following verbs in the pluperfect subjunctive passive.

1. **emō, emere, ēmī, emptum**, to buy

ego _____   nōs _____

tū _____   vōs _____

is _____   eī _____

2. **oblīviscor, oblīviscī, oblītus sum**, to forget

ego _____   nōs _____

tū _____   vōs _____

is _____   eī _____

Exercise 14.5

Write the following verbs in the imperfect subjunctive active in the person provided.

1. tū (permittō) _____

2. is (mīror) _____

3. nōs (putō) _____

4. eī (doleō) _____

5. vōs (simulō) _____

6. ego (habitō) _____

7. eī (navigō) _____

8. ego (soleō) _____

9. vōs (pendō) _____

10. is (fluō) _____

Exercise 14.6

Write the following verbs in the imperfect subjunctive passive in the person provided.

1. tū (arbitror) _____

2. eī (rogō) _____

3. eī (tueor) _____

4. is (fīniō) _____

5. nōs (spernō) _____

6. vōs (fungor) _____

7. ego (cūrō) _____

8. tū (mandō) _____

9. is (potior) _____

10. is (loquor) _____

Exercise 14.7

Write the following verbs in the pluperfect subjunctive active in the person provided.

1. is (accidō) _____
2. is (prōmittō) _____
3. vōs (faciō) _____
4. eī (instruō) _____
5. vōs (rumpō) _____
6. eī (interficiō) _____
7. is (dubitō) _____
8. tū (invideō) _____
9. tū (memorō) _____
10. ego (veniō) _____

Exercise 14.8

Write the following verbs in the pluperfect subjunctive passive in the person provided.

1. eī (iubeō) _____
2. is (līberō) _____
3. ego (nascor) _____
4. eī (morior) _____
5. nōs (parō) _____
6. is (teneō) _____
7. tū (petō) _____
8. nōs (inveniō) _____
9. ego (audeō) _____
10. is (confiteor) _____

Exercise 14.9

Translate the following verbs into English.

1. appārērent _____

2. prōderer _____

3. redditus essem _____

4. ornātī essent _____

5. ratī essētis _____

6. solitus essēs _____

7. tollerentur _____

8. collēgisset _____

9. complecterēmur _____

10. ingrederēminī _____

11. exuissem _____

12. precārētur _____

13. contentī essēmus _____

14. nescīvissēs _____

15. creātī essent _____

16. fluerent _____

17. sīvissem _____

18. dīligerēmur _____

19. volāvissent _____

20. ēgressī essent _____

Exercise 14.10

Translate the following verbs into Latin using the vocabulary provided.

1. he had entered (**intrō**) _____

2. they had been called (**appellō**) _____

3. you (pl.) were afraid (**vereor**) _____

4. we had sung (**cantō**) _____

5. we had begged (**precor**) _____

6. you (sing.) had been lost (**perdō**) _____

7. I was running (**currō**) _____

8. she had hesitated (**moror**) _____

9. they were cutting (**scindō**) _____

10. I was stretching (**tendō**) _____

15

Irregular Verbs

Latin has surprisingly few irregular verbs. For most, their irregularity appears only in the present tense. The perfect system tenses of all follow the regular rules.

Sum, esse, fuī, futūrus, to be, exist

indicative mood

present	*imperfect*	*future*
sum	eram	erō
es	erās	eris
est	erat	erit
sumus	erāmus	erimus
estis	erātis	eritis
sunt	erant	erunt

subjunctive mood

present	*imperfect*
sim	essem
sīs	essēs
sit	esset
sīmus	essēmus
sītis	essētis
sint	essent

The verb **sum** also appears with prefixes. The most common of these compounds are:

absum, abesse, āfuī, āfutūrus, to be away
adsum, adesse, adfuī, to be present, be nearby

Note: **fore** is an alternate form to the future infinitive active (**futūrus esse**), and with personal endings can be used for the imperfect subjunctive, for example, **forem** for **essem**, **forēs** for **essēs**, etc.

Exercise 15.1

Translate the following verbs into English.

1. eram _____

2. sim _____

3. eritis _____

4. fuit _____

5. erimus _____

6. fuistī _____

7. fuerat _____

8. fuerint _____

9. essēmus _____

10. es _____

11. erunt _____

12. sīs _____

13. est _____

14. erō _____

15. sumus _____

16. fuissem _____

17. estis _____

18. fuisse _____

19. fuissēmus _____

20. forētis _____

Exercise 15.2

Translate the following verbs into Latin using the indicative mood.

1. we will have been _____

2. they had been _____

3. they are _____

4. you (pl.) had been _____

5. I am _____

Exercise 15.3

Translate the following verbs into Latin using the subjunctive mood.

1. you (sing.) are _____

2. they had been _____

3. he was _____

4. I have been _____

5. we were _____

Possum, posse, potuī, **to be able**

The verb **possum** is a contraction of the words **potis** ("able") and **sum** ("be"). It shows most irregularity in the present tense, where the **t** of the seeming prefix **pot-** changes to an **s** in front of forms of **sum** that begin with an **s**. Elsewhere, **pot-** is attached to the forms of **sum**.

indicative mood

present	*imperfect*	*future*
possum	poteram	poterō
potes	poterās	poterīs
potest	poterat	poterit
possumus	poterāmus	poterīmus
potestis	poterātis	poterītis
possunt	poterant	poterunt

subjunctive mood

present	*imperfect*
possim	possem
possīs	possēs
possit	posset
possīmus	possēmus
possītis	possētis
possint	possent

Exercise 15.4

Translate the following verbs into English.

1. poterunt _____
2. potuērunt _____
3. potuerint _____
4. possīmus _____
5. posset _____
6. potuerās _____
7. potestis _____
8. potueris _____
9. poterit _____
10. potuissēs _____
11. poterātis _____
12. possent _____
13. posse _____
14. potuerim _____
15. potuisse _____
16. potuistī _____
17. potuissent _____
18. potestis _____
19. poterās _____
20. possum _____

Exercise 15.5

Translate the following verbs into Latin using the indicative mood.

1. we were able _____
2. you (sing.) have been able _____
3. I will have been able _____
4. they are able _____
5. he had been able _____

Exercise 15.6

Translate the following verbs into Latin using the subjunctive mood.

1. you (pl.) had been able _____

2. I have been able _____

3. he is able _____

4. you (sing.) were able _____

5. he had been able _____

Volō, velle, voluī, **to be willing, want**

The verb **volō** is highly irregular in both the present indicative and the present subjunctive. The other tenses follow the same rules for regular third conjugation verbs. It also has two important compound verbs, **nolō**, which is a contraction of **nōn** and **volō**, and **mālō**, which is a contraction of **māgis** and **volō**.

indicative mood

present	*imperfect*	*future*
volō	volēbam	volam
vīs	volēbās	volēs
vult	volēbat	volet
volumus	volēbāmus	volēmus
vultis	volēbātis	volētis
volunt	volēbant	volent

subjunctive

present	*imperfect*
velim	vellem
velīs	vellēs
velit	vellet
velīmus	vellēmus
velītis	vellētis
velint	vellent

Exercise 15.7

Translate the following verbs into English.

1. volēs _____

2. voluerimus _____

3. voluerāmus _____

4. volēbātis _____

5. voluisse _____

6. voluērunt _____

7. velit _____

8. voluerit _____

9. volent _____

10. volunt _____

11. vellet _____

12. voluissēs _____

13. voluerātis _____

14. vultis _____

15. velint _____

16. volam _____

17. voluistī _____

18. vīs _____

19. volēbās _____

20. velle _____

Exercise 15.8

Translate the following verbs into Latin using the indicative mood.

1. they will have wanted _____

2. they have wanted _____

3. we are willing _____

4. you (sing.) will want _____

5. they had wanted _____

Exercise 15.9

Translate the following verbs into Latin using the subjunctive mood.

1. you (sing.) had wanted _____

2. you (pl.) have been willing _____

3. we are willing _____

4. he was willing _____

5. they had wanted _____

Nōlō, nōlle, nōluī, not to want, to be unwilling

indicative mood

present	*imperfect*	*future*
nōlō	nōlēbam	nōlam
nōn vīs	nōlēbās	nōlēs
nōn vult	nōlēbat	nōlet
nōlumus	nōlēbāmus	nōlēmus
nōn vultis	nōlēbātis	nōlent

subjunctive mood

present	*imperfect*
nōlim	nōllem
nōlīs	nōllēs
nōlit	nōllet
nōlīmus	nōllēmus
nōlītis	nōllētis
nōlint	nōllent

imperative mood

nōlī	nōlīte

Exercise 15.10

Translate the following verbs into English.

1. nōn vīs _____

2. nōlit _____

3. nōluerit _____

4. nōlle _____

5. nōllent _____

6. nōluī _____

7. nōlēmus _____

8. nōlet _____

9. nōlumus _____

10. nōlēbam _____

11. nōluit _____

12. nōluerās _____

13. nōllet _____

14. nōluerimus _____

15. nōluissem _____

16. nōn vultis _____

17. nōlētis _____

18. nōlunt _____

19. nōluimus _____

20. nōlim _____

Exercise 15.11

Translate the following verbs into Latin using the indicative mood.

1. you (sing.) have been unwilling _____

2. we don't want _____

3. I will not want _____

4. he is unwilling _____

5. they will have been unwilling _____

Exercise 15.12

Translate the following verbs into Latin using the subjunctive mood.

1. they had not wanted _____

2. we do not want _____

3. I am unwilling _____

4. you (sing.) were unwilling _____

5. he has been unwilling _____

Mālō, mālle, māluī, to want more, prefer

indicative mood

present	*imperfect*	*future*
mālō	mālēbam	mālam
māvīs	mālēbās	mālēs
māvult	mālēbat	mālet
mālumus	mālēbāmus	mālēmus
māvultis	mālēbātis	mālent

subjunctive mood

present	*imperfect*
mālim	māllem
mālīs	māllēs
mālit	māllet
mālīmus	māllēmus
mālītis	māllētis
mālint	māllent

Exercise 15.13

Translate the following verbs into English.

1. mālam _____

2. māluerimus _____

3. māluisse _____

4. mālēbant _____

5. māluissem _____

6. mālint _____

7. māluerāmus _____

8. māvultis _____

9. māllent _____

10. māluerim _____

11. mālēbāmus _____

12. māluerās _____

13. mālent _____

14. mālunt _____

15. māvīs _____

16. māluerint _____

17. mālīmus _____

18. māluimus _____

19. mālle _____

20. mālētis _____

Exercise 15.14

Translate the following verbs into Latin using the indicative mood.

1. you (pl.) prefer _____

2. I will prefer _____

3. he has preferred _____

4. we had preferred _____

5. you (sing.) used to prefer _____

Exercise 15.15

Translate the following verbs into Latin using the subjunctive mood.

1. you (sing.) prefer _____

2. we used to prefer _____

3. they have preferred _____

4. I had preferred _____

5. he prefers _____

Eō, īre, iī or *īvī, itum,* to go

The Latin verb meaning "to go" is usually found with a prefix. Here is a list of some very common compounds:

abeō, abīre, abiī *or* abīvī, abitum, to go away
adeō, adīre, adiī *or* adīvī, aditum, to go to, approach
exeō, exīre, exiī, exitum, to go out, end
obeō, obīre, obiī *or* obīvī, obitum, to meet, die
pereō, perīre, periī, peritum, to die, go through, be lost
redeō, redīre, rediī, reditum, to go back, return

indicative mood

present	*imperfect*	*future*
eō	ībam	ībō
īs	ībās	ībis
it	ībat	ībit
īmus	ībāmus	ībimus
ītis	ībātis	ībitis
eunt	ībant	ībunt

subjunctive mood

present	*imperfect*
eam	īrem
eās	īrēs
eat	īret
eāmus	īrēmus
eātis	īrētis
eant	īrent

Note: Unlike the other irregular verbs presented earlier in this chapter, **eō** has gerund and gerundive forms.

participles

present	iēns, euntis
perfect	———
future	itūrus, -a, -um
gerundive	eundum
gerund	eundī, eundō, etc.
supine	itum

Exercise 15.16

Translate the following verbs into English.

1. īrent _____

2. redīre _____

3. exīs _____

4. obiērunt _____

5. ierint _____

6. perīrētis _____

7. exierāmus _____

8. abiērunt _____

9. ībō _____

10. redeās _____

11. adīrem _____

12. obit _____

13. redībunt _____

14. iit _____

15. abībāmus _____

16. exierat _____

17. perībit _____

18. redivisse _____

19. adītūrus esse _____

20. eās _____

Exercise 15.17

Translate the following verbs into Latin using the indicative mood.

1. they will go (**eō**) _____

2. he will have returned (**redeō**) _____

3. they have died (**obeō**) _____

4. we are going out (**exeō**) _____

5. I used to go (**eō**) _____

Exercise 15.18

Translate the following verbs into Latin using the subjunctive mood.

1. you (sing.) were returning (**redeō**) _____

2. they had approached (**adeō**) _____

3. he is leaving (**exeō**) _____

4. we have gone (**eō**) _____

5. I had gone away (**abeō**) _____

Ferō, ferre, tulī, lātum, to carry, bring, bear, endure

Ferō is irregular only in the forms presented below. All other forms follow the pattern of a regular third conjugation verb.

present indicative

active	*passive*
ferō	feror
fers	ferris
fert	fertur
ferimus	ferimur
fertis	feriminī
ferunt	feruntur

present infinitive

active	*passive*
ferre	ferrī

imperative

singular	*plural*
fer	ferte

Exercise 15.19

Translate the following verbs into English.

1. lātus esset _____
2. ferrer _____
3. tuleram _____
4. fertur _____
5. ferrī _____
6. tuleritis _____
7. ferēris _____
8. ferimus _____
9. lātī sunt _____
10. ferāmur _____
11. ferēs _____
12. fers _____
13. lātī sint _____
14. tulisset _____
15. ferimur _____
16. ferrēminī _____
17. tuleris _____
18. feruntur _____
19. ferāmus _____
20. ferēbat _____

Exercise 15.20

Translate the following verbs into Latin using the indicative mood.

1. he will carry _____
2. they were being carried _____

3. you (sing.) are being carried _____

4. you (pl.) will have carried _____

5. I had carried _____

Exercise 15.21

Translate the following verbs into Latin using the subjunctive mood.

1. you (pl.) had been carried _____

2. she has been carried _____

3. they had carried _____

4. I was being carried _____

5. you (sing.) are carrying _____

Fīō, fierī, factus sum, to be made, be done, be, become, happen

The verb **fīō** is not irregular in form so much as it is peculiar. While it has some active voice uses, it is also used as the passive for the verb **faciō**. Its forms, on the other hand, are strictly active in the present system tenses and passive in the perfect system.

indicative mood

present	*imperfect*	*future*
fīō	fīēbam	fīam
fīs	fīēbās	fīēs
fit	fīēbat	fīet
fīmus	fīēbāmus	fīēmus
fītis	fīēbātis	fīētis
fīunt	fīēbant	fient

subjunctive mood

present	*imperfect*
fīam	fierem
fīās	fierēs
fīat	fieret
fīāmus	fierēmus
fīātis	fierētis
fīant	fierent

Exercise 15.22

Translate the following verbs into English.

1. fiō _____

2. factus erit _____

3. fiunt _____

4. fīēbam _____

5. fiant _____

6. factī sumus _____

7. fieret _____

8. factī essētis _____

9. factī sint _____

10. fiet _____

11. fierent _____

12. factus sīs _____

13. factī erimus _____

14. fīēbant _____

15. fīs _____

16. factī essent _____

17. factus esse _____

18. fīmus _____

19. facta est _____

20. fīēbās _____

Exercise 15.23

Translate the following verbs into Latin using the indicative mood.

1. I am becoming _____

2. you (sing.) were becoming _____

3. he will have become _____

4. you (pl.) had become _____

5. they will become _____

Exercise 15.24

Translate the following verbs into Latin using the subjunctive mood.

1. you (pl.) were becoming _____

2. you (sing.) have become _____

3. we are becoming _____

4. I had become _____

5. they are becoming _____

Answer Key

Exercise 2.1

1. spērō, spērās, spērat, spērāmus, spērātis, spērant
2. vocō, vocās, vocat, vocāmus, vocātis, vocant
3. sustineō, sustinēs, sustinet, sustinēmus, sustinētis, sustinent
4. praebeō, praebēs, praebet, praebēmus, praebētis, praebent

Exercise 2.2

1. laudāmus
2. iacēs
3. latētis
4. volant
5. cantant
6. indicātis
7. nominō
8. optātis
9. putō
10. mandō
11. ornās
12. memorāmus
13. terret
14. meret
15. expectātis
16. habet
17. vetāmus
18. pateō
19. dubitātis
20. existimās

Exercise 2.3

1. he is preparing
2. they are washing
3. they are sailing
4. they are hurting
5. you (pl.) are destroying
6. they are pleasing
7. you (sing.) are carrying
8. they are in the habit of
9. she is doing nothing
10. I am asking
11. he is awake
12. she is taking care of
13. you (sing.) are working
14. you (pl.) are showing
15. he is ruling
16. I am answering
17. she is hoping
18. you (pl.) are living
19. he is staying
20. they are calling back

Exercise 2.4

1. dant
2. mutat
3. necās
4. postulāmus
5. ambulās
6. docētis
7. donant
8. vocās
9. stāmus
10. retinēmus

Exercise 3.1

1. canō, canis, canit, canimus, canitis, canunt
2. currō, curris, currit, currimus, curritis, currunt

3. accipiō, accipis, accipit, accipimus, accipitis, accipiunt
4. conficiō, conficis, conficit, conficimus, conficitis, conficiunt
5. inveniō, invenīs, invenit, invenīmus, invenītis, inveniunt

Exercise 3.2

1. aspicis
2. crescō
3. clauditis
4. regis
5. noscit
6. caedunt
7. consulitis
8. caedit
9. mittimus
10. revertō
11. contemnis
12. fundō
13. colit
14. vincitis
15. fingimus
16. conficiunt
17. gerunt
18. neglegimus
19. accidit
20. petit

Exercise 3.3

1. she is selling
2. they are surrounding
3. he is cherishing
4. they are taking
5. I am writing
6. she is escaping
7. she is continuing
8. you (pl.) are guarding
9. I am joining
10. they are opening up

11. we are losing
12. it is flowing
13. we are envying
14. he is leaving
15. she is buying
16. they are putting
17. I am finishing
18. they are fortifying
19. we are sparing
20. you are accepting

Exercise 3.4

1. relinquit
2. impōnō
3. pervenīmus
4. dūcitis
5. fīgunt
6. iaciunt
7. spargunt
8. vīvis
9. veniō
10. eripimus
11. descendunt
12. frangis

Exercise 4.1

1. impōnēbam, impōnēbās, impōnēbat, impōnēbāmus, impōnēbātis, impōnēbant
2. sciēbam, sciēbās, sciēbat, sciēbāmus, sciēbātis, sciēbant
3. regnābam, regnābās, regnābat, regnābāmus, regnābātis, regnābant
4. nocēbam, nocēbās, nocēbat, nocēbāmus, nocēbātis, nocēbant

Exercise 4.2

1. comparābat
2. intrābant
3. mittitis
4. movēbat

5. nesciēbātis
6. condēbam
7. imperābās
8. muniēbat
9. sepeliēbāmus
10. claudēbam
11. stābāmus
12. dūcēbās
13. intendēbant
14. rīdēbant
15. permittēbam
16. scrībēbāmus
17. superābātis
18. committēbās
19. fluēbant
20. negābat

Exercise 4.3

1. they were denying
2. she was singing
3. you (pl.) were throwing
4. I was hitting
5. you (sing.) were filling up
6. you (pl.) were praising
7. he was hoping
8. I was giving birth
9. she was breathing
10. you (pl.) were destroying
11. he was playing
12. they were being harmful
13. she was meeting
14. you (pl.) were preparing
15. I was hurrying
16. we were entrusting
17. you (pl.) were killing
18. he was choosing
19. we were loosening
20. you (pl.) were consulting

Exercise 4.4

1. statuēbātis
2. addēbās
3. debēbāmus
4. dīligēbās
5. donābat
6. promittēbātis
7. ēveniēbat
8. revocābant
9. dubitābam
10. accipiēbam

Exercise 5.1

1. aperiam, aperiēs, aperiet, aperiēmus, aperiētis, aperient
2. merēbō, merēbis, merēbit, merēbimus, merēbitis, merēbunt
3. pugnābō, pugnābis, pugnābit, pugnābimus, pugnābitis, pugnābunt
4. ascendam, ascendēs, ascendet, ascendēmus, ascendētis, ascendent

Exercise 5.2

1. dormiētis
2. rogābunt
3. vīvam
4. ignorābimus
5. augēbunt
6. discedēmus
7. intelleget
8. noscam
9. quaerētis
10. neglegēmus
11. reget
12. cernēmus
13. perveniam
14. cognoscētis
15. spargēmus
16. accipiam
17. defendet

18. dolēbitis
19. horrēbimus
20. continēbunt

Exercise 5.3

1. they will carry
2. we will walk
3. I will warn
4. you (pl.) will sing
5. you (pl.) will make known
6. she will buy
7. he will stay
8. we will drink
9. you (pl.) will withdraw
10. you will kill
11. she will turn back
12. you (sing.) will open
13. they will stand
14. you (pl.) will have
15. I will take
16. he will think
17. they will approach
18. I will do
19. they will build
20. we will fight

Exercise 5.4

1. ascendet
2. cōnicient
3. laedam
4. merēbunt
5. sūmēmus
6. expectābis
7. līberābimus
8. postulābunt
9. retinēbitis
10. aspicient

Exercise 6.1

1. sumpsī, sumpsistī, sumpsit, sumpsimus, sumpsistis, sumpsērunt

2. sumpseram, sumpserās, sumpserat, sumpserāmus, sumpserātis, sumpserant

3. sumpserō, sumpseris, sumpserit, sumpserimus, sumpseritis, sumpserint

Exercise 6.2

1. accidī
2. agitāvistī
3. armāvī
4. effūgistis
5. trādidit
6. cēpērunt
7. exercuistis
8. rūpimus
9. tenuistī
10. frēgērunt

Exercise 6.3

1. pepercerat
2. petierāmus/petīverāmus
3. sēderant
4. sprēverātis
5. custōdierat/custōdīverat
6. cinxerāmus
7. fūderam
8. requīsierant/requīsīverant
9. sustulerās
10. ceciderat

Exercise 6.4

1. invēneritis
2. portāverit
3. presseris
4. servīverit
5. vēnerint
6. recēperimus

7. aluerint

8. cecīderō

9. tetenderimus

10. audīveritis

Exercise 6.5

1. I thought

2. she believed

3. they will have placed

4. I will have put

5. he gathered

6. we had strained

7. you (pl.) were awake

8. she had deceived

9. he swore

10. I had envied

11. we will have found

12. they called

13. they helped

14. they had announced

15. you (pl.) exposed

16. she will have begun

17. you (pl.) covered

18. you grabbed

19. I mixed

20. we conquered

Exercise 6.6

1. strāveritis

2. laborāverās

3. mutāverant

4. existimāvistī

5. narrāvērunt

6. pandī

7. cessāverāmus

8. confēcerat

9. cucurrit

10. instituerātis
11. valueram
12. vexerit
13. appellāverō
14. iunxistis
15. praebuerint

Exercise 7.1

1. optor, optāris, optātur, optāmur, optāminī, optantur
2. caveor, cavēris, cavētur, cavēmur, cavēminī, caventur
3. contemnor, contemneris, contemnitur, contemnimur, contemniminī, contemnuntur
4. excipior, exciperis, excipitur, excipimur, excipiminī, excipiuntur

Exercise 7.2

1. induēbar, induēbāris, induēbātur, induēbāmur, induēbāminī, induēbantur
2. lavābar, lavābāris, lavābātur, lavābāmur, lavābāminī, lavābantur
3. respiciēbar, respiciēbāris, respiciēbātur, respiciēbāmur, respiciēbāminī, respiciēbantur

Exercise 7.3

1. sustinēbor, sustinēberis, sustinēbitur, sustinēbimur, sustinēbiminī, sustinēbuntur
2. tangar, tangēris, tangētur, tangēmur, tangēminī, tangēntur
3. fīniar, fīniēris, fīniētur, fīniēmur, fīniēminī, fīnientur

Exercise 7.4

1. parcitur
2. petimur
3. iubentur
4. sperniminī
5. custōdīris
6. cingimur
7. relinquor
8. requiruntur
9. tolleris
10. cupitur

Exercise 7.5

1. pōnēbar
2. agitābāris
3. amābar
4. muniēbaminī
5. trādēbatur
6. capiēbantur
7. exercēbāminī
8. rumpēbāmur
9. tenēbāris
10. frangēbantur

Exercise 7.6

1. inveniēminī
2. portābitur
3. premēris
4. iaciētur
5. sepelientur
6. recipiēmur
7. monēbuntur
8. caedar
9. tendēmur
10. audiēminī

Exercise 7.7

1. I was being ruled
2. they will be prepared
3. it was being entered
4. you (pl.) will be sent
5. he is being moved
6. it is being founded
7. we are being fortified
8. they will be buried
9. it is being closed
10. you (sing.) will be led

11. you are being led
12. I am being allowed
13. they were being written
14. she is being overcome
15. you (sing.) were being connected
16. we are being thrown
17. she will be beaten
18. it will be filled up
19. you (sing.) will be praised
20. we are being destroyed

Exercise 7.8

1. lūdēbāminī
2. mandātur
3. necāberis
4. legar
5. solventur
6. consulēbāmur
7. addētur
8. dīligeris
9. defendor
10. cūrābiminī

Exercise 8.1

1. debitus sum, debitus es, debitus est, debitī sumus, debitī estis, debitī sunt
2. factus sum, factus es, factus est, factī sumus, factī estis, factī sunt

Exercise 8.2

1. empta sum, empta es, empta est, emptae sumus, emptae estis, emptae sunt
2. gesta sum, gesta es, gesta est, gestae sumus, gestae estis, gestae sunt

Exercise 8.3

1. nōtus eram, nōtus erās, nōtus erat, nōtī erāmus, nōtī erātis, nōtī erant
2. apertus eram, apertus erās, apertus erat, apertī erāmus, apertī erātis, apertī erant

Exercise 8.4

1. ostentum eram, ostentum erās, ostentum erat, ostenta erāmus, ostenta erātis, ostenta erant
2. collectum eram, collectum erās, collectum erat, collecta erāmus, collecta erātis, collecta erant

Exercise 8.5

1. sītus erō, sītus eris, sītus erit, sītī erimus, sītī eritis, sītī erunt
2. retentus erō, retentus eris, retentus erit, retentī erimus, retentī eritis, retentī erunt

Exercise 8.6

1. caesī estis
2. petītus es
3. dīvīsī sunt
4. sprētus es
5. custōdītī estis
6. lectī sumus
7. laudātus est
8. occupātī sunt
9. sublātus est
10. receptī sunt

Exercise 8.7

1. posita eram
2. līberāta erās
3. factae erant
4. trāditae erātis
5. trādita erat
6. iactae erant
7. sprēta eram
8. victae erāmus
9. aucta erās
10. rupta erat

Exercise 8.8

1. inventus erit
2. portātī eritis
3. pressus eris

4. iactī eritis

5. sepultī erunt

6. receptī erimus

7. monitī erunt

8. caesī erimus

9. tentus erō

10. audītus erit

Exercise 8.9

1. we had been conquered

2. you (sing.) were loved

3. you (pl.) will have been made strong

4. it had been drunk

5. I was taken

6. we will have been helped

7. she had been heard

8. they were changed

9. they will have been created

10. he was dressed

11. they had been pushed

12. it was raised

13. you (sing.) will have been killed

14. I had been understood

15. she was hurt

16. you (pl.) will have been enlarged

17. they had been carried

18. it was broken

19. they will have been cut

20. I will have been added

Exercise 8.10

1. vīsus sum

2. audītī eritis

3. addītum erat

4. negāta est

5. nescītum erat

6. falsus eram
7. fīnītī erunt
8. ductī estis
9. revocātus es
10. acceptī erimus

Exercise 9.1

1. lābor, lāberis, lābitur, lābimur, lābiminī, lābuntur
2. precor, precāris, precātur, precāmur, precāminī, precantur

Exercise 9.2

1. ausa sum, ausa es, ausa est, ausae sumus, ausae estis, ausae sunt
2. experta sum, experta es, experta est, expertae sumus, expertae estis, expertae sunt

Exercise 9.3

1. ultum eram, ultum erās, ultum erat, ulta erāmus, ulta erātis, ulta erant
2. cunctātum eram, cunctātum erās, cunctātum erat, cunctāta erāmus, cunctāta erātis, cunctāta erant

Exercise 9.4

1. patiar, patiēris, patiētur, patiēmur, patiēminī, patientur
2. tuēbor, tuēberis, tuēbitur, tuēbimur, tuēbiminī, tuēbuntur

Exercise 9.5

1. morātī estis
2. secūtus es
3. cunctātī sunt
4. mortuus es
5. questus sum
6. functī sumus
7. conātus est
8. ūsī sunt
9. imitātus est
10. frūctī sumus

Exercise 9.6

1. mīror
2. arbitrāris
3. potiuntur
4. patiminī
5. expereris
6. oriuntur
7. hortor
8. consequimur
9. irasceris
10. tuētur

Exercise 9.7

1. profecta est
2. ēgressae erātis
3. ingressa erās
4. nāta eram
5. aggressae erant
6. locūtae erāmus
7. pollicitae erant
8. confessae erāmus
9. oblīta eram
10. gāvīsa erat

Exercise 9.8

1. rēbāris
2. mentiēbātur
3. verēbantur
4. lābēbāmur
5. ulciscēbar
6. precābantur
7. complectēbar
8. morābāminī
9. ūtēbātur
10. mīrābātur

Exercise 9.9

1. she had gone out
2. you (pl.) will have performed
3. they had suffered
4. he is delaying
5. I was born
6. we will have forgotten
7. they were confessing
8. you (pl.) were approaching
9. they will die
10. he will acquire
11. she had followed
12. they are avenging
13. you (sing.) were thinking
14. you (sing.) will think
15. you (sing.) used
16. he will have stepped in
17. he is embracing
18. you (sing.) marvel at
19. I was pursuing
20. she rejoiced

Exercise 9.10

1. experīmur
2. profectus eram
3. precātī sumus
4. conābāris
5. vereor
6. locūtī erant
7. cunctābiminī
8. moriēbātur
9. tuēbitur
10. hortābātur

Exercise 10.1

1. aperiēns/—; —/apertus; apertūrus/aperiendus
2. augēns/—; auctus/—; auctūrus/augendus

3. indicāns/—; —/indicātus; indicātūrus/indicandus

4. iaciēns/—; —/iactus; iactūrus/iaciendus

5. constituēns/—; —/constitūtus; constitutūrus/constituendus

Exercise 10.2

1. —, regnandī, regnandō, regnandum, regnandō

2. —, ardendī, ardendō, ardendum, ardendō

3. —, parcendī, parcendō, parcendum, parcendō

4. —, capiendī, capiendō, capiendum, capiendō

5. —, inveniendī, inveniendō, inveniendum, inveniendō

Exercise 10.3

1. rejoicing
2. about to be/must be walked
3. about to be/must be struggled
4. about to hesitate
5. about to be/must be remembered
6. about to spare
7. conquered
8. about to run
9. about to prepare
10. completing
11. speaking
12. about to/must confess
13. about to mix
14. denied
15. about to be/must be begun
16. rising
17. about to be earned
18. feared
19. scattered
20. shaping

Exercise 10.4

1. tenēns
2. petītus

3. pugnandus

4. revocātus

5. contemnens

6. doctūrus

7. vīvens

8. ferendus

9. retentus

10. flētūrus

Exercise 11.1

1. parē, parēte, nolī parēre, nolīte parēre

2. caede, caedite, nolī caedere, nolīte caedere

3. scī, scīte, nolī scīre, nolīte scīre

4. recipe, recipite, nolī recipere, nolīte recipere

5. negā, negāte, nolī negāre, nolīte negāre

6. fac, facite, nolī facere, nolīte facere

7. fer, ferte, nolī ferre, nolīte ferre

8. audē, audēte, nolī audēre, nolīte audēre

9. verēre, verēminī, nolī verērī, nolīte verērī

10. conāre, conāminī, nolī conārī, nolīte conārī

Exercise 11.2

1. build!

2. accept!

3. spread!

4. destroy!

5. don't recline!

6. follow!

7. enter!

8. don't try!

9. don't lead!

10. think!

Exercise 11.3

1. occupāte

2. nolīte induere

3. pervenī

4. nolī irascī

5. solve

Exercise 12.1

1. perdere/perdī; perdidisse/perditus esse; perditūrus esse/perditum īrī

2. invenīre/invenīrī; invēnisse/inventus esse; inventūrus esse/inventum īrī

3. monēre/monērī; monuisse/monitus esse; monitūrus esse/ monitum īrī

4. parere/parī; peperisse/partus esse; partūrus esse/ partum īrī

5. armāre/armārī; armāvisse/armātus esse; armātūrus esse/armātum īrī

Exercise 12.2

1. to have caused

2. not to be known

3. to have been chosen

4. to attack

5. to be about to be armed

6. to have stayed

7. to be eager

8. to be about to take

9. to be about to fly

10. to bathe

11. to have conquered

12. to have connected

13. to be believed

14. to be helped

15. to be about to be cut

16. to have welcomed

17. to have loved

18. to kill

19. to have been killed

20. to have been pushed

Exercise 12.3

1. bibitūrus esse

2. profectus esse

3. properāre

4. timēre
5. creārī
6. percussus esse
7. precārī
8. ratus esse
9. dīctum īrī
10. implētūrus esse

Exercise 13.1

1. neglegam, neglegās, neglegat, neglegāmus, neglegātis, neglegant
2. amem, amēs, amet, amēmus, amētis, ament
3. fugiam, fugiās, fugiat, fugiāmus, fugiātis, fugiant
4. videam, videās, videat, videāmus, videātis, videant

Exercise 13.2

1. laedar, laedāris, laedātur, laedāmur, laedāminī, laedant
2. specter, spectēris, spectētur, spectēmur, spectēminī, spectentur
3. ulciscar, ulciscāris, ulciscātur, ulciscāmur, ulciscāminī, ulciscantur
4. mentiar, mentiāris, mentiātur, mentiāmur, mentiāminī, mentiantur

Exercise 13.3

1. texerim, texeris, texerit, texerimus, texeritis, texerint
2. vēnerim, vēneris, vēnerit, vēnerimus, vēneritis, vēnerint

Exercise 13.4

1. fūsus sim, fūsus sīs, fūsus sit, fūsī sīmus, fūsī sītis, fūsī sint
2. questus sim, questus sīs, questus sit, questī sīmus, questī sītis, questī sint

Exercise 13.5

1. colligās
2. crescat
3. cēdāmus
4. trādant
5. existiment
6. relinquam

7. āmittant

8. cessem

9. colātis

10. exerceat

11. temptēs

12. respiciant

13. celebret

14. figāmus

15. sentiat

Exercise 13.6

1. comparēris

2. quaerantur

3. querāminī

4. reperiāmur

5. agitēminī

6. aspiciāmur

7. custōdiantur

8. lauder

9. horter

10. sustineātur

11. institutāris

12. reddātur

13. polliceātur

14. apellētur

15. oriantur

Exercise 13.7

1. mīseritis

2. cēpērunt

3. posuerit

4. postulāverit

5. ēgeritis

6. patuerit

7. traxerimus

8. didicerint

9. gesserim

10. ostenderimus

Exercise 13.8

1. ēgressus sim
2. vocātī sītis
3. additī sint
4. datus sit
5. falsī sītis
6. imitātus sīs
7. lūsī sint
8. raptus sit
9. morātus sim
10. mutātus sit

Exercise 13.9

1. it being finished
2. you (sing.) are cherishing
3. I was on guard
4. I am persuading
5. they are serving
6. you (pl.) are being consulted
7. we worked
8. they are writing
9. I am embracing
10. he lacked
11. she was divided
12. they were joined
13. you (sing.) are desiring
14. you (pl.) are announcing
15. they are being buried
16. we are being allowed
17. you (sing.) harmed
18. you (pl.) are being heard
19. he is being stretched
20. they were deceived

Exercise 13.10

1. vehar
2. soleās

3. experiāminī
4. habitent
5. dēfenderimus
6. reversī sint
7. canat
8. tactus sīs
9. mīrāta sit
10. mortuī sint

Exercise 14.1

1. cernerem, cernerēs, cerneret, cernerēmus, cernerētis, cernerent
2. narrārem, narrārēs, narrāret, narrārēmus, narrārētis, narrārent

Exercise 14.2

1. fruerer, fruerēris, fruerētur, fruerēmur, fruerēminī, fruerentur
2. fīnīrer, fīnīrēris, fīnīrētur, fīnīrēmur, fīnīrēminī, fīnīrentur

Exercise 14.3

1. latuissem, latuissēs, latuisset, latuissēmus, latuissētis, latuissent
2. intrāvissem, intrāvissēs, intrāvisset, intrāvissēmus, intrāvissētis, intrāvissent

Exercise 14.4

1. emptus essem, emptus essēs, emptus esset, emptī essēmus, emptī essētis, emptī essent
2. oblītus essem, oblītus essēs, oblītus esset, oblītī essēmus, oblītī essētis, oblītī essent

Exercise 14.5

1. permitterēs
2. mīrāret
3. putārēs
4. dolērent
5. simulārētis
6. habitārem
7. navigārent

8. solērem
9. penderētis
10. flueret

Exercise 14.6

1. arbitrārēris
2. rogārentur
3. tuērentur
4. fīnīrētur
5. spernerēmur
6. fungerēminī
7. cūrārer
8. mandārēris
9. potīrētur
10. loquerētur

Exercise 14.7

1. accidisset
2. prōmīsisset
3. fēcissētis
4. instruxissent
5. rūpissētis
6. interfēcissent
7. dubitāvisset
8. invīdissētis
9. memorāvissētis
10. vēnissem

Exercise 14.8

1. iussī essent
2. līberātus esset
3. nātus essem
4. mortuī essent
5. parātī essēmus
6. tentus esset
7. petītus essēs

8. inventī essēmus

9. ausus essem

10. confessus esset

Exercise 14.9

1. they were appearing
2. I was being betrayed
3. I had been given back
4. they had been decorated
5. you (pl.) had judged
6. you (sing.) had been accustomed
7. they were being carried
8. she had collected
9. we were embracing
10. you (pl.) were entering
11. I had stripped
12. he was begging
13. we had been hurried
14. you had not known
15. they had been created
16. they were flowing
17. I had allowed
18. we were being loved
19. they had flown
20. they had gone out

Exercise 14.10

1. intrāvisset
2. appellātī essent
3. verērēminī
4. cantāvissēmus
5. precātī essēmus
6. perditus essēs
7. currerem
8. morāta esset
9. scīnderent
10. tenderem

Exercise 15.1

1. I was
2. I am
3. you (pl.) will be
4. he has been
5. we will be
6. you (sing.) have been
7. she had been
8. they will have been *or* they have been
9. we were
10. you are
11. they will be
12. you are
13. he is
14. I will be
15. we are
16. I had been
17. you (pl.) are
18. to have been
19. we had been
20. you (pl.) were

Exercise 15.2

1. fuerimus
2. fuerant
3. sunt
4. fuerātis
5. sum

Exercise 15.3

1. sīs
2. fuissent
3. esset
4. fuerim
5. essēmus

Exercise 15.4

1. they will be able
2. they were able
3. they will have been able *or* they have been able
4. we are able
5. she was able
6. you (sing.) had been able
7. you (pl.) are able
8. you (sing.) will have been able *or* you (sing.) have been able
9. he will be able
10. you (sing.) had been able
11. you (pl.) had been able
12. they were able
13. to be able
14. I have been able
15. to have been able
16. you (sing.) have been able
17. they had been able
18. you (pl.) are able
19. you (sing.) were able
20. I am able

Exercise 15.5

1. poterāmus
2. potuistī
3. potuerō
4. possunt
5. potuerat

Exercise 15.6

1. potuissētis
2. potuī
3. possit
4. possēs
5. potuisset

Exercise 15.7

1. you (sing.) will want
2. we will have wanted *or* we have wanted
3. we had wanted
4. you (pl.) were wanting
5. to have wanted
6. they have wanted
7. she wants
8. he will have wanted *or* he has wanted
9. they will want
10. they want
11. she was wanting
12. you (sing.) had wanted
13. you (pl.) had wanted
14. you (pl.) want
15. they want
16. I will want
17. you (sing.) have wanted
18. you (sing.) want
19. you (sing.) were wanting
20. to want

Exercise 15.8

1. voluerint
2. voluērunt
3. volumus
4. volēs
5. voluerant

Exercise 15.9

1. voluissēs
2. volueritis
3. velimus
4. vellet
5. voluissent

Exercise 15.10

1. you (sing.) don't want
2. she doesn't want
3. he will not have wanted *or* he has not wanted
4. to not want
5. they didn't want
6. I have not wanted
7. we will not want
8. she will not want
9. we do not want
10. I was not wanting
11. he has not wanted
12. you (sing.) had not wanted
13. she was not wanting
14. we will not have wanted *or* we have not wanted
15. I had not wanted
16. you (pl.) do not want
17. you (pl.) will not want
18. they do not want
19. we have not wanted
20. I do not want

Exercise 15.11

1. nōluistī
2. nōlumus
3. nōlam
4. nōn vult
5. nōluerint

Exercise 15.12

1. nōluissent
2. nōlīmus
3. nōlim
4. nōllēs
5. nōluerit

Exercise 15.13

1. I will prefer
2. we will have preferred *or* we have preferred
3. to have preferred
4. they were preferring
5. I had preferred
6. they prefer
7. we had preferred
8. you (pl.) prefer
9. they were preferring
10. I have preferred
11. we were preferring
12. you (sing.) had preferred
13. they will prefer
14. they prefer
15. you (sing.) prefer
16. they will have preferred *or* they have preferred
17. we prefer
18. we have preferred
19. to prefer
20. you (pl.) will prefer

Exercise 15.14

1. māvultis
2. mālam
3. māluit
4. mālueram
5. mālēbās

Exercise 15.15

1. mālīs
2. māllēmus
3. māluerint
4. māluissem
5. mālit

Exercise 15.16

1. they were going
2. to go back
3. you (sing.) are going out
4. they have met
5. they will have gone *or* they have gone
6. you (pl.) were dying
7. we had gone out
8. they have gone away
9. I will go
10. you are going back
11. I was going to
12. he is meeting
13. they will go back
14. she has gone
15. we were going away
16. he had gone out
17. she will die
18. to have gone back
19. to be about to go to
20. you are going

Exercise 15.17

1. ībunt
2. redierit
3. obiērunt
4. exīmus
5. ībam

Exercise 15.18

1. redīrēs
2. adiissent
3. exeat
4. ierimus
5. abiissem

Exercise 15.19

1. he had been carried
2. I was being carried
3. I had carried
4. he is being carried
5. to be carried
6. you (pl.) will have carried *or* you (pl.) have carried
7. you (sing.) will be carried
8. we are carrying
9. they have been carried
10. we are being carried
11. you (sing.) will carry
12. you are carrying
13. they have been carried
14. he had carried
15. we are being carried
16. you (pl.) were being carried
17. you (sing.) will have carried *or* you (sing.) have carried
18. they are being carried
19. we are carrying
20. she was carrying

Exercise 15.20

1. feret
2. ferēbantur
3. ferris
4. tuleritis
5. tuleram

Exercise 15.21

1. lātī essēs
2. lāta sit
3. tulissent
4. ferrer
5. ferās

Exercise 15.22

1. I am becoming
2. he will have become
3. they are becoming
4. I was becoming
5. they are becoming
6. we have become
7. he was becoming
8. you (pl.) had become
9. they have become
10. he will become
11. they were becoming
12. you (sing.) have become
13. we will have become
14. they were becoming
15. you (sing.) are becoming
16. they had become
17. to have become
18. we are becoming
19. she has become
20. you (sing.) were becoming

Exercise 15.23

1. fīō
2. fīēbās
3. factus erit
4. factī erātis
5. fīent

Exercise 15.24

1. fierent
2. factus sīs
3. fīāmus
4. factus essem
5. fīant

Index of Latin Verbs

abeō, abīre, abiī *or* abīvī, abitum, to go away

absum, abesse, āfuī, āfutūrus, to be away

accēdō, accēdere, accessī, accessum, to approach, go near (with *ad* or *in* and the accusative)

accidō, accidere, accidī, to happen, fall down, ask for help

accipiō, accipere, accēpī, acceptum, to welcome, receive

addō, addere, addidī, additum, to add, give to

adeō, adīre, adiī *or* adīvī, aditum, to go to, approach

adsum, adesse, adfuī, adfutūrus to be present, be nearby

aggredior, aggredī, aggressus sum, to approach, attack

agitō, agitāre, agitāvī, agitātum, to agitate, think about, get something going

agō, agere, ēgī, actum, to do, drive, lead, be busy

alō, alere, aluī, altum, cherish, nourish

ambulō, ambulāre, ambulāvī, ambulātum, to walk

āmittō, āmittere, āmīsī, āmissum, to send away, let go, lose

amō, amāre, amāvī, amātum, to like, love

aperiō, aperīre, aperuī, apertum, to open, uncover

appāreō, appārēre, appāruī, appāritum, to appear

appellō, appellāre, appellāvī, appellātum, to call (often by name)

arbitror, arbitrārī, arbitrātus sum, to think

ardeō, ardēre, arsī, arsum, to burn, be on fire

armō, armāre, armāvī, armātum, to equip with weapons

ascendō, ascendere, ascendī, ascensum, to climb, go up

aspiciō, aspicere, aspexī, aspectum, to look at

audeō, audēre, ausus sum, to dare

audiō, audīre, audīvī, audītum, to hear, listen

augeō, augēre, auxī, auctum, to increase, enlarge

bibō, bibere, bibī, bibitum, to drink

cadō, cadere, cecidī, cāsum, to fall

caedō, caedere, cecīdī, caesum, to cut, kill

canō, canere, cecinī, cantum, to sing, play (an instrument)

cantō, cantāre, cantāvī, cantātum, to sing, play (an instrument)

capiō, capere, cēpī, captum, to take, catch

careō, carēre, caruī, caritūrus, to lack, be without (uses an ablative object)

caveō, cavēre, cāvī, cautum, to beware, be on guard

cēdō, cēdere, cessī, cessum, to go, withdraw, yield

celebrō, celebrāre, celebrāvī, celebrātum, to visit often, make well known

cernō, cernere, crēvī, crētum, to separate, distinguish, pick out

certō, certāre, certāvī, certātum, to struggle, decide by contest

cessō, cessāre, cessāvī, cessātum, to do nothing, slack off

cingō, cingere, cinxī, cinctum, to surround, wrap

claudō, claudere, clausī, clausum, to close, conclude

cōgitō, cōgitāre, cōgitāvī, cōgitātum, to think, ponder

cognoscō, cognoscere, cognōvī, cognitum, to learn; (in the perfect system) to know

cōgō, cōgere, coēgī, coactum, to compel, gather, drive, force

colligō, colligere, collēgī, collectum, to gather, collect

colō, colere, coluī, cultum, to pay attention to, nurture, cultivate

comedō, comedere, comēdī, comēsum *or* comestum, to eat up

committō, committere, commīsī, commissum, to connect, combine; entrust

comparō, comparāre, comparāvī, comparātum, to prepare, buy, furnish

complector, complectī, complexus sum, to hug, embrace

condō, condere, condidī, condītum, to found, build; put in safe keeping, hide

conficiō, conficere, confēcī, confectum, to finish

confiteor, confitērī, confessus sum, to confess, admit

cōniciō, cōnicere, cōniēcī, cōniectum, to hurl

conor, conārī, conātus sum, to try, attempt

consequor, consequī, consecūtus sum, to follow, pursue, obtain

constituō, constituere, constituī, constitūtum, to stand or set something up, decide

constō, constāre, constitī, constātum, to stand together, stand still, stop

consulō, consulere, consuluī, consultum, to consult

contemnō, contemnere, contempsī, contemptum, to despise

contendō, contendere, contendī, contentum, to strain, hurry, fight

contineō, continēre, continuī, contentum, to hold together, contain

crēdō, crēdere, crēdidī, crēditum, to trust, rely on, believe (usually with dative)

creō, creāre, creāvī, creātum, to create, elect

crescō, crescere, crēvī, crētum, to grow

cunctor, cunctārī, cunctātus sum, to hesitate, delay

cupiō, cupere, cupīvī, cupītum, desire, long for

cūrō, curāre, curāvī, curātum, to take care of

currō, currere, cucurrī, cursum, to run

custōdiō, custōdīre, custōdiī *or* custōdīvī, custōdītum, to guard

debeō, debēre, debuī, debitum, to owe; ought, should, must

dēfendō, dēfendere, dēfendī, dēfensum, to defend, drive off

dēleō, dēlēre, dēlēvī, dēlētum, to destroy

descendō, descendere, descendī, descensum, to climb down

dīcō, dīcere, dīxī, dīctum, to tell, say

dīligō, dīligere, dīlexī, dīlectum, to love, esteem, pick out

discedō, discedere, discessī, discessum, to leave, separate

discō, discere, didicī, to learn

dīvidō, dīvidere, dīvīsī, dīvīsum, to divide

dō, dare, dedī, datum, to give

doceō, docēre, docuī, doctum, to teach

doleō, dolēre, doluī, dolitum, to feel pain, to cause pain

donō, donāre, donāvī, donātum, to give (as a gift)

dormiō, dormīre, dormīvī, dormītum, to sleep

dubitō, dubitāre, dubitāvī, dubitātum, to hesitate, doubt

dūcō, dūcere, duxī, ductum, to take someone someplace, lead

effugiō, effugere, effūgī, to escape

ēgredior, ēgredī, ēgressus sum, to leave, go out

emō, emere, ēmī, emptum, to buy

eō, īre, iī *or* īvī, itum, to go

ēripiō, ēripere, ēripuī, ēreptum, to grab, to take out violently

errō, errāre, errāvī, errātum, to wander, be wrong

ēveniō, ēvenīre, ēvēnī, ēventum, to come out, result

excipiō, excipere, excēpī, exceptum, to take out, take up, catch, receive

exeō, exīre, exiī, exitum, to go out, end

exerceō, exercēre, exercuī, exercitum, to make strong, train, harass

existimō, existimāre, existimāvī, existimātum, to think, judge, evaluate

exuō, exuere, exuī, exūtum, to strip

experior, experīrī, expertus sum, to try, test, prove

exspectō, exspectāre, exspectāvī, exspectātum, to wait for

faciō, facere, fēci, factum, to make, do

fallō, fallere, fefellī, falsum, to deceive

ferō, ferre, tulī, lātum, to carry, bring, bear, endure

fīgō, fīgere, fixī, fixum, to fasten, affix

fingō, fingere, finxī, fictum, to shape, form

fīniō, fīnīre, fīnīvī, fīnītum, to finish

fīō, fierī, factus sum, to be made, be done, be, become, happen (used for passive of faciō)

fleō, flēre, flēvī, flētum, to weep

fluō, fluere, fluxī, fluxum, to flow

frangō, frangere, frēgī, fractum, to break

fruor, fruī, fructus sum, to enjoy (usually with ablative)

fugiō, fugere, fūgī, fugitum, to run away, flee

fundō, fundere, fūdī, fūsum, to pour

fungor, fungī, functus sum, to perform (usually with ablative)

gaudeō, gaudēre, gāvīsus sum, to rejoice, be happy

gerō, gerere, gessī, gestum, to carry, accomplish, wear (clothes)

gignō, gignere, genuī, genitum, to give birth, cause

habeō, habēre, habuī, habitum, to have, hold, consider, regard

habitō, habitāre, habitāvī, habitātum, to live, dwell, inhabit

horreō, horrēre, horruī, to bristle

hortor, hortārī, hortātus sum, to encourage, urge

iaceō, iacēre, iacuī, to recline, lie

iaciō, iacere, iēcī, iactum, to throw

ignōrō, ignōrāre, ignōrāvī, ignōrātum, to not know

imitor, imitārī, imitātus sum, to copy

imperō, imperāre, imperāvī, imperātum, to give an order (with dative object)

impleō, implēre, implēvī, implētum, to fill up

impōnō, impōnere, imposuī, impositum, to put upon

incipiō, incipere, incēpī, inceptum, to begin

indicō, indicāre, indicāvī, indicātum, to make known, betray

induō, induere, induī, indūtum, to put on, dress

ingredior, ingredī, ingressus sum, to step in, begin

instituō, instituere, instituī, institūtum, to set up, instruct, decide

instruō, instruere, instruxī, instructum, to build, equip

intellegō, intellegere, intellexī, intellectum, to understand, be aware of, appreciate

intendō, intendere, intendī, intentum, to stretch, intend, aim at

interficiō, interficere, interfēcī, interfectum, kill

intrō, intrāre, intrāvī, intrātum, to enter

inveniō, invenīre, invēnī, inventum, to come upon, find

invideō, invidēre, invīdī, invīsum, to cast the evil eye, envy (with dative)

irascor, irascī, irātus sum, to become angry

iubeō, iubēre, iussī, iussum, to order

iungō, iungere, iunxī, iunctum, to join, connect

iūrō, iūrāre, iūrāvī, iūrātum, to swear

iuvō, iuvāre, iūvī, iūtum, to help, please

lābor, lābī, lapsus sum, to slip

laborō, laborāre, laborāvī, laborātum, to work, suffer

laedō, laedere, laesī, laesum, to hurt

lateō, latēre, latuī, to lie hidden

laudō, laudāre, laudāvī, laudātum, to praise

lavō, lavāre, lāvī, lautum *or* lavātum *or* lōtum, to wash

legō, legere, lēgī, lectum, to choose, pick, gather, read

līberō, līberāre, līberāvī, līberātum, to set free

loquor, loquī, locūtus sum, to talk, speak

lūdō, lūdere, lūsī, lūsum, to play, deceive

mālō, mālle, māluī, to want more, prefer

mandō, mandāre, mandāvī, mandātum, to entrust, order

maneō, manēre, mansī, mansum, to stay

memorō, memorāre, memorāvī, memorātum, to remind, mention

mentior, mentīrī, mentītus sum, to lie, deceive

mereō, merēre, meruī, meritum, to deserve, earn

metuō, metuere, metuī, metūtum, to fear

mīror, mīrārī, mīrātus sum, to marvel at, wonder, be amazed

misceō, miscēre, miscuī, mixtum, to mix

mittō, mittere, mīsī, missum, to send, release, throw, to make something go away under
    its own power

moneō, monēre, monuī, monitum, to warn, advise

monstrō, monstrāre, monstrāvī, monstrātum, to show

morior, morī, mortuus sum (fut. part. moritūrus), to die

moror, morārī, morātus sum, to hesitate, delay, kill time

moveō, movēre, mōvī, mōtum, to move

mūniō, mūnīre, mūniī, mūnītum, to fortify

mutō, mutāre, mutāvī, mutātum, to change, move

narrō, narrāre, narrāvī, narrātum, to tell (in story form)

nascor, nascī, nātus sum, to be born

nāvigō, nāvigāre, nāvigāvī, nāvigātum, to sail

necō, necāre, necāvī, necātum, to kill

neglegō, neglegere, neglexī, neglectum, to neglect

negō, negāre, negāvī, negātum, to deny, say no

nesciō, nescīre, nescīvī, nescītum, to not know

noceō, nocēre, nocuī, nocitum, to harm, be harmful (with dative)

nōlō, nōlle, nōluī, not to want, to be unwilling

nōminō, nōmināre, nōmināvī, nōminātum, to name, mention

noscō, noscere, nōvī, nōtum, to learn; (in perfect system) to know, recognize

nuntiō, nuntiāre, nuntiāvī, nuntiātum, to announce

obeō, obīre, obiī *or* obīvī, obitum, to meet, die

oblīvīscor, oblīvīscī, oblītus sum, to forget (with genitive)

occīdo, occīdere, occīdī, occīsum, to kill

occupō, occupāre, occupāvī, occupātum, to seize

occurro, occurrere, occurrī, occursum, to meet (with dative)

optō, optāre, optāvī, optātum, to choose

orior, orīrī, ortus sum, to rise

ornō, ornāre, ornāvī, ornātum, to decorate

ōrō, ōrāre, ōrāvī, ōrātum, to beg, ask, speak, pray

ostendō, ostendere, ostendī, ostentum, to show

pandō, pandere, pandī, pansum *or* passum, to open up, stretch

parcō, parcere, pepercī, parsum, to spare, be sparing (with dative)

pāreō, pārēre, pāruī, pāritum, to be obedient, obey

pariō, parere, peperī, partum, to give birth, produce

parō, parāre, parāvī, parātum, to get ready, obtain, prepare

pateō, patēre, patuī, to lie open, be exposed

patior, patī, passus sum, to suffer, experience

pellō, pellere, pepulī, pulsum, to push, drive

pendō, pendere, pependī, pensum, to hang, weigh, pay

percutiō, percutere, percussī, percussum, to hit, strike

perdō, perdere, perdidī, perditum, to lose, destroy, waste

pereō, perīre, periī, peritum, to die, go through, be lost

perficiō, perficere, perfēcī, perfectum, to complete

pergō, pergere, perrexī, perrectum, to continue

permittō, permittere, permīsī, permissum, to allow, send through, throw

persuadeō, persuadēre, persuasī, persuasum, to persuade (with dative)

perveniō, pervenīre, pervēnī, perventum, to arrive

petō, petere, petiī *or* petīvī, petītum, to look for, ask, head for, attack

placeō, placēre, placuī, placitum, to please (with dative)

polliceor, pollicērī, pollicitus sum, to promise

pōnō, pōnere, posuī, positum, to put, lay

portō, portāre, portāvī, portātum, to carry, bring

possum, posse, potuī, to be able

postulō, postulāre, postulāvī, postulātum, to demand

potior, potīrī, potītus sum, to acquire

praebeō, praebēre, praebuī, praebitum, to offer
precor, precārī, precātus sum, to pray, beg
premō, premere, pressī, pressum, to press, push
prōdō, prōdere, prōdidī, prōditum, to betray, hand over
proficiscor, proficiscī, profectus sum, to set out, leave
prōmittō, prōmittere, prōmīsī, prōmissum, to promise, send ahead
properō, properāre, properāvī, properātum, to hurry
pugnō, pugnāre, pugnāvī, pugnātum, to fight
putō, putāre, putāvī, putātum, to think, value
quaerō, quaerere, quaesiī *or* quaesīvī, quaesītum, to look for, ask
queror, querī, questus sum, to complain
quiescō, quiescere, quiēvī, quiētum, to rest
rapiō, rapere, rapuī, raptum, to take (forcefully)
recipiō, recipere, recēpī, receptum, to accept, take back
recurrō, recurrere, recurrī, recursum, to run back
reddō, reddere, reddidī, redditum, to give back, surrender, repeat
redeō, redīre, rediī, reditum, to go back, return
regnō, regnāre, regnāvī, regnātum, to rule
regō, regere, rexī, rectum, to rule, guide
relinquō, relinquere, relīquī, relictum, to abandon, leave
reor, rērī, ratus sum, to think, judge
reperiō, reperīre, repperī, repertum, to find
requīrō, requīrere, requīsiī *or* requīsīvī, requīsītum, to demand, ask, look for
respiciō, respicere, respexī, respectum, to look back
respondeō, respondēre, respondī, responsum, to answer, correspond (usually with dative)
retineō, retinēre, retinuī, retentum, to hold back, keep
revertō, revertere, revertī, reversum, to turn back
revocō, revocāre, revocāvī, revocātum, to call back
rīdeō, rīdēre, rīsī, rīsum, to laugh, smile
rogō, rogāre, rogāvī, rogātum, to ask
rumpō, rumpere, rūpī, ruptum, to break, burst
scindō, scindere, scidī, scissum, to cut
sciō, scīre, scīvī, scītum, to know
scrībō, scrībere, scripsī, scriptum, to write, draw
sedeō, sedēre, sēdī, sessum, to sit, stay put
sentiō, sentīre, sensī, sensum, to feel, perceive, experience, realize
sepeliō, sepelīre, sepeliī *or* sepelīvī, sepultum, to bury
sequor, sequī, secūtus sum, to follow

servio, servīre, servīvī, servītum (with dative), to be a slave, serve

simulō, simulāre, simulāvī, simulātum, to pretend

sinō, sinere, sīvī, situm, to let, allow

soleō, solēre, solitus sum, to be in the habit of doing something, usually do something

solvō, solvere, solvī, solūtum, to loosen, untie, pay

sonō, sonāre, sonuī, sonātum, to make a sound

spargō, spargere, sparsī, sparsum, to scatter, sprinkle

spectō, spectāre, spectāvī, spectātum, to watch

spernō, spernere, sprēvī, sprētum, to reject, scorn

spērō, spērāre, spērāvī, spērātum, to expect, hope

spīrō, spīrāre, spīrāvī, spīrātum, to breathe

statuō, statuere, statuī, statūtum, to set up, stop, decide

sternō, sternere, strāvī, strātum, to spread, stretch

stō, stāre, stetī, statum, to stand, stay

studeō, studēre, studuī, to be eager, be busy with (usually with dative)

sum, esse, fuī, futūrus, to be, exist

sūmō, sūmere, sumpsī, sumptum, to take, assume

superō, superāre, superāvī, superātum, to overcome, conquer

surgō, surgere, surrexī, surrectum, to rise

suscipiō, suscipere, suscēpī, susceptum, to undertake, accept

sustineō, sustinēre, sustinuī, sustentum, to support, uphold

taceō, tacēre, tacuī, tacitum, to be quiet

tangō, tangere, tetigī, tactum, to touch

tegō, tegere, texī, tectum, to cover

temptō, temptāre, temptāvī, temptātum, to try, test

tendō, tendere, tetendī, tentum *or* tensum, to stretch, try

teneō, tenēre, tenuī, tentum, to hold, have

terreō, terrēre, terruī, territum, to scare

timeō, timēre, timuī, to be afraid, fear

tollō, tollere, sustulī, sublātum, to raise, carry away, destroy

trādō, trādere, trādidī, trāditum, to hand over, surrender

trahō, trahere, traxī, tractum, to pull, drag

tueor, tuērī, tūtus sum, to watch, protect

ulciscor, ulciscī, ultus sum, to avenge

ūtor, ūtī, ūsus sum (with ablative), to use; to benefit oneself (by means of)

valeō, valēre, valuī, valitum, to be strong

vehō, vehere, vexī, vectum, to carry; to ride (middle voice with ablative)

vendō, vendere, vendidī, venditum, to sell

venio, venīre, vēnī, ventum, to come

vereor, verērī, veritus sum, to be afraid

vertō, vertere, vertī, versum, to turn

vetō, vetāre, vetuī, vetitum, to deny, say no

videō, vidēre, vīdī, vīsum, to see; (passive voice) to seem, be seen

vigilō, vigilāre, vigilāvī, vigilātum, to be awake, watch

vincō, vincere, vīcī, victum, to conquer

vīvō, vīvere, vixī, victum, to live

vocō, vocāre, vocāvī, vocātum, to call, summon

volō, volāre, volāvī, volātum, to fly

volō, velle, voluī, to be willing, want